(1) PLAY (2)
0000 0000 0000

GAME ON

Published in 2002 by
Laurence King Publishing Ltd
71 Great Russell Street
London WC1B 3BP
T: +44 20 7430 8850
F: +44 20 7430 8880
E: enquiries@laurenceking.co.uk
www.laurenceking.co.uk

In association with the exhibition:
Game On
16 May–15 September 2002
Barbican Gallery, Barbican Centre
London EC2Y 8DS
www.barbican.org.uk

Barbican Art Galleries are
owned, funded and managed
by the Corporation of London

The Barbican would like to
thank its current Art Partners:
Linklaters, Clifford Chance,
Bloomberg, BP, Slaughter and
May, Simmons and Simmons

Commissioning Editor:
Jo Lightfoot/Laurence King Publishing
Guest Curator: Lucien King
Barbican Curator: Conrad Bodman
Exhibition Organizers:
Neil McConnon, Sophie Persson
Curatorial Assistant: Katherine Oliver

Design and art direction:
Martina Keller/Intro
Design: Simon Dovar/Intro
Co-ordination: Charlotte Dale/Intro
www.introwebsite.com

A catalogue record for this book
is available from the British Library.

ISBN 1 85669 304 X

Printed in China

CONTENTS

GAME ON FOREWORD

(1)   PLAY   (2)
0000   0000   0000
CAROL BROWN   HEAD OF ART GALLERIES
CONRAD BODMAN   CURATOR

We are entering the 40th year in the history of videogames. It is surprising therefore that this book accompanies the first exhibition covering the subject ever to be held in a UK art gallery. There is no doubt that videogames have had a significant impact on contemporary visual culture and are worthy of consideration. The *Game On* exhibition and book demonstrate the creativity of the individuals involved in game design and programming, and also explore the influence that games have had on musicians, filmmakers and contemporary artists.

Games have always been a part of human culture. No wonder then that artists have sometimes adopted a gaming mode in order not just to have fun but to challenge our perceptions. In our recent Martin Parr retrospective we included a replay of a game he made in the 1970s that we showed in 1994, *Love Cubes*. Visitors were invited to work out which of the individuals photographed on the street were, in fact, couples. The viewers' solutions said as much about themselves, surely, as the people they were looking at.

Serious Games, *The Art Casino*, and now *Game On*: all titles of exhibitions at the Barbican that have touched on gaming. *Serious Games* focused on how artists were using new technology and, in particular, audience participation in an art context. In *The Art Casino* artists explored the nature of gambling (roulette, horse racing, card playing) at a moment just before the launch of the National Lottery when there was serious debate about its inevitable impact on arts funding.

Despite all of this, *Game On* marks the first time that we have recognized the breadth of interest in games played on the computer. The exhibition and this publication confound any notion that games are about just a small sector of the public: isolated individuals (usually young men). It recognizes that computer game-playing is a worldwide phenomenon that reflects and, some say, shapes our culture.

Game On was conceived by Lucien King, who is Guest Curator of the exhibition and who has written the introduction to this book. Lucien originally convinced Mark Jones (then Director of the Museum of Scotland) to fund the initial *Game On* research. Barbican Gallery's involvement developed from a games conference called *Into the Real* held at the ICA in 2000, where Barbican Gallery's Curator Conrad Bodman (who had already been working on a similar proposal) met staff from the Museum of Scotland. The project developed in a collaborative manner with Barbican Gallery leading on the research and development of the exhibition. We are grateful to all of the people in Edinburgh who have contributed to this project from its inception, particularly Stephen Elson and Jem Fraser.

Special thanks go to the authors who have contributed new writing to this book. We would also like to thank all of the games developers, publishers, artists and collectors who have allowed their images to be used.

Carol Brown (Head of Art Galleries)
Conrad Bodman (Curator)
Barbican Art Galleries

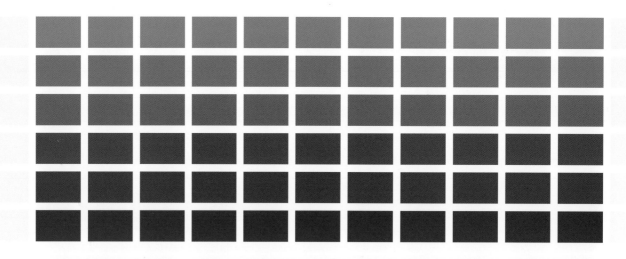

KANDAHAR

A film by Mohsen Makhmalbaf

'...vivid and memorable' *Independent*

'...at once comic, grotesque and beautiful' *Guardian*

'...haunting' *New Statesman*

'When I look into the future, I can scare myself out of optimism quite easily, much less utopianism.

I see a world where dominator politics prevail, where human rights abuses multiply in direct relation to increasing poverty and overpopulation. I see world religions in a state of rigor mortis, with a death grip on science, art, and the exchange of ideas. I see the ecology of the Alaskan Arctic devoured by petro-gluttony and the forests of Indonesia in flames. Worst of all, I see a world where people can't talk to each other in any meaningful way. Global networking will be a tool of business communication, consumerism, propaganda, banal conversations, and mindless entertainment. We will have forgotten how to tell stories or to hear them. The majority of the world's population will be very young people without extended families or intact cultures, with fanatical allegiances to dead religions or live dictatorships. We have what Jonas Salk called a "wisdom deficit" – fewer elders and even fewer people who listen to them.'

(From Brenda Laurel's *Utopian Entrepreneur*, MIT Press)

This passage from Brenda Laurel's latest book shows how important it is for us and future generations to find ways of reversing the damage we've all done to Mother Nature. A strange and depressing way to start a book dedicated to understanding the games we play, you may think. In fact it is an attempt to set a context for the writing in this collection; a realistic context which recognizes that as the world plays it must not forget the more serious business of maintaining a world where play is possible.

Humans have been building mysterious or predictable new game worlds for a long time now. For slightly less time we have been doing this electronically as well.

I've always enjoyed games, but often wonder how we can be having so much fun when substantial parts of our world are burning, drowning, disappearing?

How can we be dancing to HedKandi in Ibiza... while a particularly unfortunate Bengal tiger is skinned in its cage in a New Delhi Zoo? Reading great books like *Easy Riders, Raging Bulls* and *Such a Long Journey*? Watching super movies like *Kandahar, Shrek, Tillsammans* or *Amelie*? Spending time with precious friends and family over heaps of Hogwarts-style tucker? We've got Choice Hot 97s and Radio 4s in every town and village... radio and papers to digest and roll and recycle. So many rich avenues to fun and games.

Yet, just over there, on the other side of the 6 x Nightly News, we can all see extreme close-ups of everything that is not ideal in our world.

And still we play games. More and more it would seem. It has got to be more complicated than the pursuit of idle escapism. Hasn't it?

It was one of the first freezing nights of November 2001. Blazing hip-hop and R&B. I was walking down Holloway Road at 19:45hrs, southbound. On a bustling corner, criss-crossed by two full lanes of outbound traffic, a 17-year-old boy and a 14-year-old girl were playing kick-about with an empty bottle of Volvic… what a harsh place to find playful intent.

Despite everything that happens in the world, we continue, like they did, to play. We play to connect, to co-operate and compete, and ultimately to learn through practice. Physically and mentally we are drawn or made to play. But why?

This book is all about games of the electronic variety. We wanted to look at the global impact of games. To do this we invited people from various parts of the planet to write down some of their thoughts and ideas about what games are and what they represent to different cultures, and to suggest ways of approaching games as a subject of interest. The writers in this book are some of the people I have enjoyed talking about games with. The opportunity to collect the ideas we had discussed in book form arose out of four years of work on what will be the biggest independent show on videogame culture and history to date.

To fill in a little background to the show and the book:

It was my parents' 30th wedding anniversary, the summer of 1998.

Mark Jones, then Director of the National Museum of Scotland, was there. And we took a stroll into Bressieux, a lovely little village in the South of France.

Mark was then the proud custodian of a recently enlarged museum in Edinburgh. We discussed the fact that videogames could be seen to make more money for the Scottish economy than its oil and gas reserves put together – *if* one ignored the sad fact that most of the money Scottish games made jetted out of the country to line other nations' pockets. It was already clear that the international game market was growing faster than any other entertainment sector, and that games were a massive business. You know, all the usual headline-grabbing information about games!

Mark liked the idea of an exhibition on games and their history and culture. A lot of young people only visit museums and galleries on school or college trips. The National Museum of Scotland had been seeking ways of attracting young people back of their own accord. So we started planning a show called *Game On*, a working title which just stuck.

As we worked on how best to organize and describe the global culture and history of games, it became clear that this show was threatening to become the biggest and most expensive exhibition the museum had ever planned. We needed a partner to share the risk. So we called up Conrad Bodman, a curator at the Barbican Art Galleries in London. The Barbican had just had great success with a show called *The Art of Star Wars*, which looked at the creative practice and individuals behind the *Star Wars* phenomenon. The Barbican was trying to broaden its appeal to people who thought it was solely a gallery space for the more traditional arts. With these recent ambitions and experiences, the team at the Barbican was perfectly set up for organizing a major show on videogames.

We had the venues and the budgets and development teams. The biggest arts centre in Europe and the National Museum of Scotland were going to open their hallowed halls to game culture. How cool was that? This was going to be an important opportunity for games to shine in the cultural spotlight, not just for being big moneyspinners for hardened capitalists, but as a valuable aspect of our social lives.

COMPUTER
SPACE

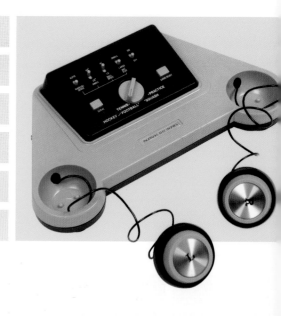

Opposite page
top left

PDP-1 computer
1962

This page

The Magnavox
Odyssey flyer

Opposite page
top right

Ingersoll *Pong*
console, 1976

Opposite page
bottom

Computer Space
1971

We developed an outline which gave us some sense of the scale and scope of our ambitions. This scale has remained pretty much as it was at the first few meetings in Edinburgh many moons ago. Then, of course, came the all-important content. What were people going to see and do when they came to the show?

The object list grew like a constantly updated piece of shareware. We instituted open standards from the earliest days. This show was meant to be a show for the kids of all ages who played, and made games, and for those who wanted to understand them a little better, so it needed to reflect as many ideas from those kinds of people as possible. We wanted to trace a broad historical arc following the life of games, from their birth on the PDP-1 computer in the science and research labs of the United States out into the public domain of bars and then arcades. From the hands of Nolan Bushnell and his crew – who gave us the obscure game play of *Computer Space*, followed by the pure game play of *Pong* – to the flood of *Pong* clones. Whilst the world went to war, suffered from famines and we continued to exhaust our fish stocks, some very clever people made micro-computing do ingenious and comparatively inexpensive things, which brought us the highs and lows of console gaming. Games fell into the sticky hands and cluttered bedrooms and living rooms of the world at large. In this book, Jeremy, Gautam, Alice and Mazzi all write about their personal experience of games as they first encountered them and grew up with them.

Now games are to be found as electronic extensions of our physical and mental selves, as mobile gaming platforms to be played anywhere, by anyone who can afford them. There's an intriguing four-decade circularity in finding *Space Invaders* being played on a cell phone in Dunfermline at wireless game developer Digital Bridges. Wireless games are getting deeper and broader with each new iteration. The artists and code-meisters working on the next generation of games are just as focused, able and aspirational as the generations of creative and technical wizards before them who sought to turn coded language and numbers into a playable universe of fun and emotion.

Opposite page
bottom

Retro Ex
one of the few UK
retro game shops

Opposite page
top

Taskforce
by Chu

This page

Adventure Vision
1982

Within this book, as in the show, we wanted to look to the future. We wanted to try and pick out certain trends in content and technical development, which would reveal future directions for gaming. This is where the interesting stuff needs to happen, the developments that will drag games out of the lucrative niche they currently inhabit – predominantly defined by young men, for boys. No cultural phenomenon can multiply its effect without seeking to broaden its reach. So we, as game designers, need to listen to and act on the calls to become much more relevant to many more people.

Throughout all this history of the hardware and software, we wanted to highlight as many aspects of international gaming culture, well-known or otherwise, as we could in one book.

If, as I hope, *Game On* has taken the shape and dynamism it should have, it is down to the help of many people from all over the place who have given their time and knowledge freely. Thanks are due to them. Research trips throughout the UK and to Europe, Japan and the United States have been undertaken in order to do this book justice. But what about other areas of the world, areas like Africa, Palestine, the Middle East, Latin America, even India and China; regions where at least two billion of the planet's six billion possible games players live? These are some of the biggest and most diverse parts of the world. In games marketing and sales departments, so often, all these areas of our world are rounded up as R.O.W. – Rest of the World. In this book, and as much as possible within the exhibition, we seek to address and reflect these countries, in the hope of encouraging an even brighter, more representative, more imaginatively diverse future for games. Games are dreamt up, sold, bought and played on whatever market is the nearest and most economical. For many millions of us, games are part of our lifestyle – even if we don't always play them. We live in one worldwide game nation.

In order to represent, we are still travelling. Still looking, at best, like 18th-century naturalists searching for those special new species in the Amazon that only the indigenous or the well-travelled are familiar with. At worst, looking like anoraks digging around the dusty crates of time immemorial in some dank basement of a shop in Shepherd's Bush. We are looking for things we can bring back to light, and luckily, we have found many individuals and groups who have been doing the job of museums for the last forty years. We have been looking for the obvious as well as those exceptional and precious gem-like games. The book conveys some of the details and insights garnered from this four-year quest. We've been procuring the objects and contacting the people associated with them who can help explain where these games have come from – who is responsible and what they, and their games, represent. The essays aim to go behind the hype, behind the scenes, to uncover new reactions and approaches to games and entertainment.

GAME ON ⓑ

Opposite page
Jak and Daxter

This page left
**Virgin Megastore
London
Underground
poster**

This page right
Game On
**exhibition postcard
designed by State**

Games, like music, cinema and the theatre, are experiences we can share. This sharing – the handing back and forth of ideas, some of which come from the energy of youth and some of which arise through age and experience – is important to society. I can just picture an older lady and her young granddaughter shooting the breeze about the good old days when they first encountered electronic entertainment – a mere thirty-five years apart. Perhaps *Frogger* for one and *Jak and Daxter* for the other. If there is, as Brenda Laurel suggests, a 'wisdom deficit' between generations, then surely these new conversations about old and not so old experiences that we have shared can start to open more channels for inter-generational communication. The wisdom deficit cuts both ways: the old can learn from the young as much as the other way round – we have to strive harder to make all voices equally heard.

Some weeks on from when I am writing this, the book will have gone on sale and the show will have opened. The show will have enjoyed the life of a modern videogame in the way that it was conceived and developed, in the time it took and how much it has cost. Like any good game, the show builds on the work of many others, including those individuals and institutions that have seen the sense of trying to do interesting exhibitions on games before. Whether it was the American Museum of the Moving Image in Queens, NYC, or the ComputerSpieler Museum in Berlin or the Kobe Fashion Museum in Japan – we have benefited no end from your experiences and insights. This show and book are a continuation of your hard work.

If the show and its associated strands and events can be construed as the proverbial game, then this book is the game manual. Hopefully it is at least as interesting as most game manuals – lots of text certainly, but lots of big colour images to goggle at as well. There's a lot to say, and we certainly haven't said it all. Games are now Public Enemy's *Nation of Millions* with at least a million voices. We have room for only 14 here so for now this collection is meant to be a primer for those interested in games. The contributions represent the individual thoughts of those that wrote them. This is not magazine editorial – it is not really a formal book. It's conceived of more as a compendium. Dip into it chapter by chapter, in whatever order you choose. I often start at the back hoping for a summary. You won't find one at the end of this selection. Games and the writing about them is ongoing....

This is how it breaks down:

Introduction: you just about finished it!

'Violence and the Political Life of Videogames': Clive is a fellow you can have many interesting chats with. We had a couple of pints of Guinness at his local in Brooklyn. A few weeks later we had a couple of sakatinis on Manhattan. We wanted a piece to represent a key aspect of gaming in the USA. He obliged with a pretty cool essay about violence.

'I Love My Videogames': Gautam (G-Man) is 17. He is Indian, lives in London and loves hip-hop. He has played games since he was small and has a few interesting things to say about them – like that sometimes you love games and at other times of life they just all seem to suck.

'Pokémon as Japanese Culture?': Masuyama, Meguro born and bred, has been in it and winning it since the year dot. He knows about games and showed me an EPOC table tennis videogame which just rocked whilst I hung out with him in one of Tokyo's leafy western neighbourhoods. He writes about *Pokémon*, a game that perhaps could only ever have come from Japan.

'All Clicked Out': Mazzi is young, impulsive and knows more about Uganda than some. She has written a piece which only someone who knows about videogames could write. She says she doesn't like them and the effect they have had on some people and points out the risks associated with whiling away the hours on games.

'Report from the PAL Zone: European Games Culture': Andreas gives us a view from Europe. Mainland Europe is very different from the UK – some people, such as Charles Cecil of Revolution, suspect that the mainlanders are just 'more culturally sophisticated' than their UK cousins. We all have our views on this matter. Andreas sets the scene for the beginnings of a fuller understanding.

'My Story: Girls Playing Games': Alice used to work at Online Magic (hats off to Michael Martin and co.) in between blasting men at *Quake*. Now she runs her own company which helps build communities online – and still has crystal tips about why and how to enjoy games. She's got some sound advice for those involved in making and marketing games. Pay attention those of you still confused by gender and games.

'Broads, a Bitch, Never the Snitch': I have never met Jeremy – a wild man based in Canada, living it large, making it happen. He has played the games of life – no surprise that videogames have featured in amongst all that. He and Justin, who did the fly artworks which colour their contribution, get my full respect for just telling us how it is. And particularly, how it was for them.

'The Art of Contested Spaces': last time we saw Henry Jenkins and his crew at MIT it was September 11th 2001. Say no more. Henry and Kurt Squire bring some dignity to these proceedings. Sharp fellows, if for no other reason than that they have found a way to incorporate games into their department's studies. MIT, like many universities and seats of learning around the world, is finding that games have a place alongside the arts, humanities and sciences. Special shout out to Alex, Alice, Zhan, Heather and all at MIT Comparative Media.

'Character Forming': Steven knows an awful lot about games and what they might mean – but then, he knows a lot about a lot of things. He has dealt with character here in this collection – but there are many interesting observations he has to make in the future. So look out for them. He is still Trigger Happy.

'Gaming the System: Multi-player Worlds Online': JC is a native New Yorker – even though I think she moved there from somewhere else. She is involved with some serious projects and it is great to be able to include some of her collected thoughts here. She discusses the 'social ecology of gaming' – sounds very grown up but it all began with representing and trying to define a Joystick Nation.

This page and
opposite page

VIP Lounge for
Q Magazine
December 2001

'Telefragging Monster Movies': Katie is currently writing a book on game design with co-contributor Eric Z. That subject had been my first suggestion as an area she might find interesting to deal with here. But we agreed movies and games and the new dark arts of Machinima would be a better fit for us both. Machinima is new and emergent… and threatens to put more means of production into the hands of the many rather than just the professional few. That always threatens some kind of revolution! We will wait to see if this application of technology can help tell new stories in exciting new ways.

'Story as Play Space: Narrative in Games': I met Celia Pearce and Robert Nideffer at E3 2001 in LA. Not only were they full of ideas and help but, later, Celia agreed to find time in a hectic schedule to pen a think-piece on narrative. She should know – she has been studying this for ages – so we are very pleased to have her contribution in here.

'Do Independent Games Exist?': Eric has some funky offices just north of Canal in the heart of Chinatown in NYC. His office is full of all kinds of great 'old skool' and new games. But Eric is doing his own independent thing with the crew at GameLab and forward thinkers Shockwave and Lego. Two or more views of the same situation can be differing and not mutually exclusive. He presents an either/or approach as to whether games are suffering or benefiting from their current state of play. And rightly invites you to make up your own mind.

'Head Games: The Future of Play': you should all read Mark's book *The Playful World*. I finished it at 35,000 feet on the way to Tokyo a while back – it was so full of energy and actual, practical hope that we had to have him in here. He has some clear ideas about what might be upcoming in the near future – which is already in some ways our past.

This collection is really just a launch pad into the wider world of games. There are many people writing and talking about them out there. And many other voices that still need to be heard. More and more will be. We have learnt a lot from Steven Kent, the Diberdier Brothers, *myvideogames.com* and all those others who in different ways have helped start a library on games. Soon in the bookstores you won't have to struggle to find books on games. Supply will foment demand, which will demand supply, in a virtuous cycle. We just have to hope games get better and appeal to and represent broader interests and aspirations.

The games business has survived a very turbulent transitional phase these last couple of years as hardware has relentlessly continued to upgrade. There were game market crashes of sorts in 1976, 1983 and 1996 – that's one almost each decade – when the markets were forced to dramatically adapt to changing circumstances. We will have to wait and see whether the patterns of history can be resisted. Powerful forces are at work. Will this latest period of struggle have been worth it for the majority? There are signs that possibly it will. In the same way as a rebalancing took place between artist, publisher and distributor in music and movies and television and radio as they matured, so there is an ongoing re-adjustment as artists in games seek a better deal, and the publishers and distributors become ever less distinguishable. Hopefully, as these artists get more powerful, they will be freer to delight us and surprise our kids in ways we still can't even dream of.

I hope you enjoy dipping your toes into these pooled writings on games…

LJK
Pimlico, London

※

✳CLIVE THOMPSON✳

When I met David Grossman, he handed me a gun – and told me I'd probably make a good killer.

He ought to know. Three years ago, Grossman became one of the most famous proponents of the idea that videogames cause violence. He's the respected author of *On Killing* (1995), a book on the psychological aspects of killing. Most specifically, he has studied the ways that the American police force and army train their recruits to use deadly force by having them practise using videogame-like point-and-shoot devices, known as Fire Arms Training Simulators (FATS). It's this constant practising of repetitive firing that allows police to overcome the innate human distaste for taking human life – something that kept firing rates as low as 15 per cent in the First and Second World Wars. What B. F. Skinner called 'operative conditioning' is at the heart of how, since Vietnam, the American armed forces have learned to kill.

But here's the rub: Grossman argues that videogames are thus equally dangerous. Arcade and console titles like the *House of the Dead* or *Time Crisis* series, with their plastic gun pointers, are eerily exact replicas of the FATS trainers. If the desensitizing conditioning happens to police when simulations are used intentionally, it could just as easily happen unintentionally, as kids and adults play endless hours of gun-mounted first-person shooters. Children are learning to kill from videogames 'much the same way as the astronauts on Apollo 11 learned how to fly to the moon without ever leaving the ground', as Grossman later wrote.

Grossman says proof of this was provided by the wave of school shootings in recent years, in which the youthful killers have displayed unnerving accuracy with guns. One child, 14-year-old Michael Carneal, fired eight times and hit eight children when he opened fire on a prayer group at his school in 1997; a 100 per cent hit ratio. In contrast, police officers can often only manage a hit ratio of less than half that – which means that Carneal, and other game-playing teenagers like him, must be learning their marksmanship skills somewhere.

Ever since the 1999 high-school shootings in Columbine, Grossman has been popular in media circles, arguing constantly that games are to blame. So I decided to test his hypothesis. I was a useful control group; I'd played point-and-shoot games my whole life, yet never held or shot a real gun. I offered him a challenge: I'd meet him at a shooting range, and shoot a pistol for the first time – aiming for the death spots on human targets. If he was right, I'd be a natural killer. He agreed and, when we met, set me up with a heavy .45 Magnum pistol. 'Go ahead and fire,' he said.

This page and opposite page

Max Payne™

When I met David
Grossman, he handed
me a gun – and
told me I'd probably
make a good killer.

This page and opposite page
SWAT 3

It used to be that TV was the corroding influence turning Americans into mindless drones. But in the last two decades, that mantle has decisively been passed to videogames. Indeed, despite the wide variety of digital games, and the fact that the most popular genres tend to be non-violent mind puzzles (like Microsoft's *Minesweeper*, probably the most-played game in existence), violence is the issue by which the mainstream knows games. Fans would prefer it not be so, but it doesn't matter. While game designers and theorists debate frame rates or narrative or polygon counts, few in the public sphere could care less. For them, games have only one political face, one major social issue: violence. Violence tracks the political life of games.

Yet, considering its importance to game culture, the debate moves like a glacier – receding two steps for every step it goes forward. Part of the reason for this is the political blinders that many of its participants wear. Anti-violence advocates – like Grossman, and the many anti-gaming 'family-values' organizations – are political actors, fighting for their own authority in the court of the media; it's not necessarily in their interest to present all the evidence openly. And game designers and publishers are hardly any better. They nakedly market their most torridly intense titles to children well below the age of 17, while cynically claiming they'd never do such a thing. Caught in a game of snarling, mutually assured destruction, neither camp is particularly committed to understanding how games genuinely affect people. Both, however, assume that they know what's correct – that games either brainwash us into violence, or are harmless fantasies.

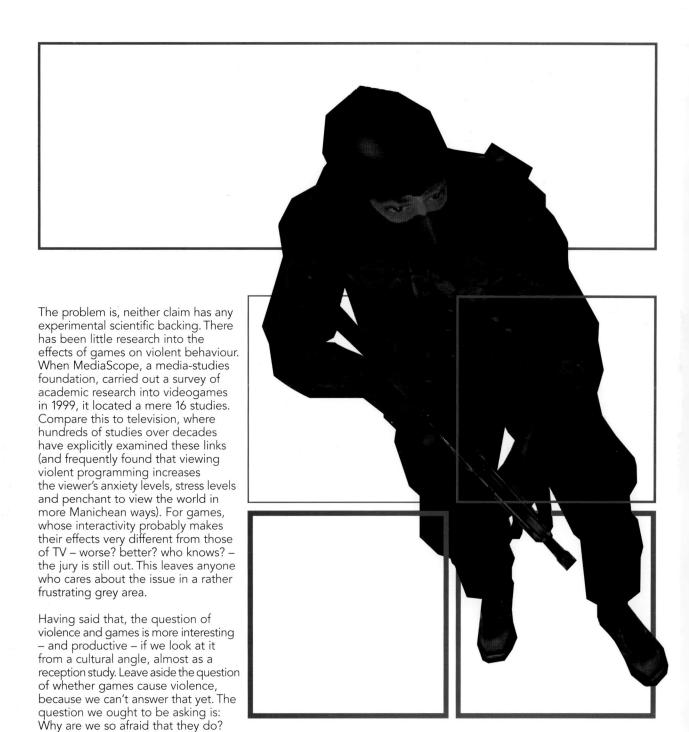

The problem is, neither claim has any experimental scientific backing. There has been little research into the effects of games on violent behaviour. When MediaScope, a media-studies foundation, carried out a survey of academic research into videogames in 1999, it located a mere 16 studies. Compare this to television, where hundreds of studies over decades have explicitly examined these links (and frequently found that viewing violent programming increases the viewer's anxiety levels, stress levels and penchant to view the world in more Manichean ways). For games, whose interactivity probably makes their effects very different from those of TV – worse? better? who knows? – the jury is still out. This leaves anyone who cares about the issue in a rather frustrating grey area.

Having said that, the question of violence and games is more interesting – and productive – if we look at it from a cultural angle, almost as a reception study. Leave aside the question of whether games cause violence, because we can't answer that yet. The question we ought to be asking is: Why are we so afraid that they do?

In the United States, certainly, it would be easy to argue that real-life guns are a far more pressing problem than virtual ones; several hundred children are killed in gun accidents in their own homes, usually because of improperly stored firearms – far more than in the last decade of school shootings. So what is it that drives observers and critics so singularly berserk about digital violence? What does this tell us about our cultural reactions to, our misinterpretations of, interactive media?

Look closely, and much of this debate comes down to identity – and how digital media lets people adopt new ones. Theorists like Sherry Turkle have for years argued that the primary social power of computers and online communities is in letting people try on new personalities. And indeed the panic over the Internet and computers in general – with the supposed platoons of hidden, anonymous cybercriminals waiting to lure children away – maps pretty closely onto videogame paranoia. What's scary may simply be the idea of people messing around with powerful new identities.

This page
Chris Redfield
Resident Evil

Opposite page
Half-Life

MIT media theorist Henry Jenkins has noted that Western culture has long had an uneasy relationship to role-playing in general. The theatre has struggled with this stigma for millennia; Socrates, for one, sought to ban it from his Republic, because he thought that pretending to be someone else was morally dishonest. Mid-second-millennium British royalty was so concerned about the theatre that, for centuries, plays could only take place with royal assent (as in Shakespeare's 'King's Players'). Nor is this merely the madness of pre-Enlightenment kooks in the past; even up until the 1960s, the Lord Chamberlain's Office in Britain had the job of reading each new play before it was allowed to be performed and determining whether it was obscene. In this context, it's easy to see why games are a lightning rod – particularly the benighted 'first-person shooter', which most dramatically puts the player into the role of the game.

Yet when you look at the games themselves, and the roles that gamers adopt, it's harder to make a case that they're manuals for social riot. Quite the contrary. As J. C. Herz first noted in her 1997 book *Joystick Nation*, games most frequently have gamers acting in the roles of forces of social order – like police (*Max Payne™*, *SWAT*), or soldiers of some vaguely defined military (*Half-Life*, the *Quake* series, the *Resident Evil* franchise). Indeed, only a vanishingly small fraction – like *Kingpin*, *Grand Theft Auto* and *Postal* – ever dare to have you act as criminals or psychopaths. On the contrary, titles like *SWAT* are all about quelling social disturbances, and they all generally evince an almost freakishly craven attitude towards authority and policing in general.

One could just as easily be worried about these games making players more likely to be patriotic hawks, blindly supporting America's military forays around the world – which are taking on positively videogame-like qualities themselves. Or, in contrast, one could reasonably wonder about how these games reflect our social attitudes towards violent policing. Shouldn't the family-values camp be a bit more concerned about, say, the fact that games seem to promote the idea that the primary activity of law enforcement is pumping endless rounds of ammunition into vermin-like criminals?

'Isolation' is the other main bugbear, the constant companion of violence in this games debate. Critics of games inevitably focus on their observation that games lock players into their own narrow world, rendering them incapable of dealing with other people. Violence is seen as an offshoot of a socially unprepared child (or adult, for that matter) encountering the messy grey areas of a real world for which they have no training. It's a stereotype that, again, maps over perfectly from the high-tech world, where programmers and geeks have long been erroneously assumed to be anti-social creeps. In fact, studies of programmer culture – beginning with Gerald M. Weinberg's seminal 1971 book *The Psychology of Computer Programming* – have usually found that programmer culture is highly verbal and networked. It has become even more so with the emergence of the Internet, which made such massively collaborative projects as *Linux* possible. Gaming has almost precisely the same social vibe. Clustering in online discussion forums, trading playing strategies in FAQs of byzantine complexity and migrating heavily to multi-player arenas in the last five years, players use games in much the same way as adult men use pro sports. Sure, it's an activity in and of itself, but it's covertly – and even overtly – a socializing device.

None of these observations, of course, can resolve the unanswered question about whether games cause aggressive behaviour. But when we look at the larger social panic over violence in this way, it's easier to see its faint reefer-madness quality. The critics rarely display any serious understanding of the culture of gamers. Instead, the focus is really ultimately on youth, and it evinces a pretty distrustful, fearful view of it; left to their own cultural devices, it seems, those kids will kill us all. This isn't a new idea, of course; in the 14th-century *Canterbury Tales*, Chaucer portrays students almost exclusively as charlatans, thieves and rapists. Rock and roll, too, was supposed to produce a generation of anarchists, when in reality it helped shape a demographic bulge of boomer materialists the likes of which America has never seen. You could easily argue that digital games are following a similar trajectory. They might seem rebellious and edgy, but they also neatly train kids in the all-American art of consumption as experience: shove another dollar into the machine, pay for yet more entertainment.

Opposite page
Grand Theft Auto III

This page
Grand Theft Auto III
Box cover artwork

Opposite page
Postal Dude
Postal

This page
Postal

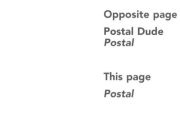

All of which brings me back to the gun range with Grossman. After he gave me the fire-away command, I pulled dutifully away on the .45, pumping dozens of rounds into the paper human targets. In one sense, it was completely unlike a videogame: the gun was heavier, the noise more extreme, the smell of gunpowder weirdly distracting, not to mention that I was truly panicked about holding a lethal weapon in my hands. But when the dust settled, it appeared that I was indeed a pretty good shot, despite never having handled a real pistol before. I'd landed about half my bullets in the centre of the chest – something that a police trainee can usually only do after a week of intensive training. Games, it seems, had given me some of the technical ability necessary to become a killer.

Still, I'd been mulling over all these issues, and wondering about all the cultural drivers that Grossman's theory left out. Certainly, it seemed plausible that point-and-shoot games might hone the physical skills needed to help me shoot a real gun. They might also help train me in the tactical aspects of mass murder – such as using only one bullet per victim, instead of firing wildly, to preserve ammunition. But even if I could embark on a killing spree, why would I want to? Eye–hand co-ordination is one thing; seething rage is quite another. The psychological roots of violence are so manifold that it seems almost surreal that games should have become a dominant player in the American debate over why people kill people. In the end, the gaming-and-violence debate is more important for what it tells us about the issues that surround it: our relationship to media, the weirdness of identity in the interactive age and the way society deals with youth. In this game, there's endless ammunition; digital entertainment will be on the firing range for years to come.

Clive Thompson

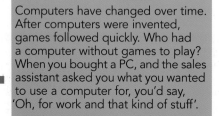

Computers have changed over time. After computers were invented, games followed quickly. Who had a computer without games to play? When you bought a PC, and the sales assistant asked you what you wanted to use a computer for, you'd say, 'Oh, for work and that kind of stuff'.

The next day, you'd open the huge boxes, and set up the computer. You would then start it up and mess around with it, going through the manuals. Time passed and you'd get bored with the computer, so you would go to the PC shop and pick up some games. You thought to yourself: 'Oh, it's just for fun; one game won't hurt'. At home you opened the computer game box with excitement as if it was a Christmas present.

You sit there with a full jug of coffee. You start playing the game and the hours fly by, then sweat starts running down your neck! You look at the clock: it's 3am. You've been playing the game all night. You think to yourself: 'I'll stop playing after the next go'. But no, your eyes go red. The coffee jug that was once full is now empty.

Welcome to the life of a gamer. Sleepless nights are common. Your chair replaces your bed. The habitual flicker of the monitor punctuates your dreams. You dream games, you wake to play games, you long for more games – you can't live without games.

I remember the Sega Master System – it was a kick-ass machine. It didn't have wicked graphics, but it had some amazing games, classics like *Desert Strike* and *Space Harrier*. In *Desert Strike* you were in control of a helicopter. You could blow up buildings from the comfort of a chair – with just your two fingers. Then there was Michael Jackson's *Moonwalker*. Based on the movie, the game was addictive. The music quality was what made it stand out from its competitors. Previously most games had lame music or no music; this game had good music and good game play. And another thing I liked about it is that you could transform from Michael into a robot. That was cool. When you changed into a robot, you got a robot's weapons.

The Sega Mega Drive improved game graphics. One amazing game on it was *Micro Machines 2* which deprived me of sleep. I used to invite friends over and play. With the potential to have up to five players, the Sega Mega Drive was a party box and videogames became a shared activity.

These days you can play Mega Drive games on the Internet: you can download the games (a.k.a. ROM files), but before you start you have to download an application (in computer speak it's called an emulation program). I recommend 'meka'. To get the emulation and ROMs, go to *www.emurater.com*. Some other good ROMs sites are *www.freeroms.com* and *www.geocities.com/snappa_fcw/ sega.html*.

The next thing to have was the Sony PlayStation. At first I thought it was all hype, just a gimmick. How wrong I was. The first game I played on it was *Need For Speed II*. When I popped the CD in, I was expecting just another car game. But I was wrong. The cars were the stuff of every young man's dream. And you didn't just get to drive them, you found out every detail about them and saw live-action footage of them babies in action. You didn't just drive in dull places, you drove on tracks based on real places around the world. I think that EA Sports make the best sports games around.

Then the Dreamcast came out. Everyone was saying it was 'the bomb'. *Soul Calibur* is an amazing fight-'em-up game. The Dreamcast was the first game system to offer an Internet connection. (Oh great, another bill to pay.)

But then some lame games came out on it. So I went to my room, dusted the dirt off my Sega Mega Drive, found a second-hand shop and got a load of games. (A good place to get second-hand games is *www1.cex.co.uk/default.asp*.) Anyway, time passed and I was getting bored of videogames. That is, until I found *Age of the Empires*, which brought out the megalomaniac in me. I was building empires, I was the king of kings, the greatest emperor ever. (Well, I think so.)

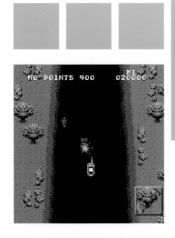

Opposite page
Moonwalker

This page left
Spy Hunter arcade,
1983

This page right
Spy Hunter console
version, 2001

One thing I noticed is that they were re-releasing old games on these new consoles. Take *Spy Hunter*, for example. The game was born on the arcade machine in 1983, became a huge hit and was put on various game machines. It was born again in 2001 on the PlayStation 2 – given a facelift that Michael Jackson would be jealous of. The game is now in 3D and it's as addictive as ever. (You can play the arcade version on the Internet *www.shockwave.com/sw/content/spyhunter.*)

But I continued to go back and forth from India to the UK, and I got bored of videogames. Nearly all the games revolved around graphics, not game play. Plus they were hard, when what I wanted was a game that was easy-but-a-bit-hard. My parents found it annoying that I was playing violent games. In India you wouldn't play violent games, you would play chess or another type of board game [falls asleep], maybe even read a book! [&*%^@ books!]. Parents in India thought videogames made you lazy; they would nag you to do your homework, and you would be like, 'Yes, I will after this one game'. But you didn't go and do your homework, you kept on playing, and later if you did work, you would be thinking about them games. But many Indian kids don't like the killing games, they prefer games like *Final Fantasy VII* that involve some thought.

Then again, we teenagers love a little shoot-'em-up [evil laugh] like *The House of the Dead 2* or *Time Crisis II*. But they were in the arcades where you had to pay £1 a game, so after some counselling I stopped playing them. Then I started getting into hip-hop, thanks to 2pac and his lyrics. I got into different artists and started bumping hip-hop 24/7. Games were less appealing as I could not relate to them; music was something I could relate to. I guess I was growing up. Most games have crap soundtracks, and some don't have any at all. But things are changing, for example *Grand Theft Auto III* has eight hours of music with rappers' songs such as 'Royce DA 5'9'. Guru the rap master is also in the game as the character 8 Ball. And when the game comes out on the PC you'll be able to get live radio feeds when you're playing [sweet]. (You can download the first Grand Theft Auto at *www.freeloader.co.uk.*)

Other popular games are sports games. Parents hate them! They are seriously addictive, you can be playing them for hours on end. Take *NHL 2000*. I can't play ice hockey, but I love the game and I find myself playing it when I'm bored. The reason why parents hate it is that playing for consecutive hours is bad for you. You don't run, you just sit there glued to the screen.

When I heard that *Grand Theft Auto III* was coming out, I played it and got hooked. The first one was amazing. The second one wasn't that bad but its downside was that it focused on graphics, not game play, and was way too hard. Hip-hop music is an integral part of *Grand Theft III* and it is a funny game (you will find out why when you play it). You can do whatever you want in the game -- you can mug someone, steal cool cars – it's you against the police and gangs. The game has everything in it so I sit here playing it into the wee hours.

These days we are all game-obsessed – there are games on mobile phones, on nearly everything with a screen, and we just like to be players. Games are an escape to me. They take my mind off things. That's why I love them....

Gautam Narang

MASUYAMA

To understand any cultural phenomenon, it is often more enlightening to explore the context behind its conception, rather than what happened after it came onto the scene. Just what is the story behind *Pokémon*?

I work in Japan as a videogame producer. In addition, I also analyse, in a wider context, videogames as cultural phenomena. Think of me as a Hollywood producer who, as well as making films, theorizes about the social impact of film. In other countries, Japan is generally viewed as particularly adept at creating videogames, comics and animation. These, like the Sony Walkman and the Honda motorbike, are viewed as unique products of 'Japanese culture'.

However, oddly enough, the average Japanese person does not see any particular connection between Japanese culture and videogames. A simple test using a Google Japan search (*www.google.co.jp*) yielded just 66 matches for the term 'videogame' (*bideo geemu*) cross-referenced with 'Japanese culture' (*nihon bunka*). On the other hand, 'Japanese culture' and the traditional Japanese art of *Kabuki* produced 2,700 search matches

Just why is this? I would like to suggest three factors. Firstly, there are always things about ourselves that are difficult to see, unless somebody else points them out to us. For example, the game *Pachinko* is considered typically 'Japanese' by Europeans, but for the Japanese, *Pachinko* machines are so utterly commonplace that it is difficult to imagine them as culturally unique to Japan. *Kabuki*, on the other hand, used to be a popular form of culture 300 years ago, but has now become a traditional, state-supported form of high art so that the Japanese think of it as part of their cultural heritage. Secondly, most consumers in the videogame market are children, which creates the idea that the games are somehow not worth mentioning or do not deserve careful examination, a tendency which is not unique to Japan. Thirdly, since the end of World War II, Japan has undergone a rapid but often superficial adoption of American culture, creating the widespread, simplistic perception that the only significant foreign culture is that of America. As a result, people believe that since videogames enjoy great popularity in both Japan and America, they must be globally universal, and that Japanese companies like Nintendo and Sega surely do not offer anything that is unique to Japan.

I wish to explore the idea of videogames as articles of Japanese culture. In particular, I wish to discuss *Pokémon*, a game that has achieved the highest global popularity of any released in the past few years. What is the game's connection to Japanese culture and what are the reasons for its incredible success?

Pokémon Red/Green was released on the Game Boy in Japan in 1996. To understand any cultural phenomenon, it is often more enlightening to explore the context behind its conception, rather than what happened after it came onto the scene. Just what is the story behind *Pokémon*? It begins as far back as the 1970s. In 1971, a game machine called *Computer Space* was set up in the corner of a bar in America's Silicon Valley. It was the world's first commercial videogame machine. Its controls were overly complex, and it certainly did not become a hit, but its existence was enough to convince game developers to begin work on the design of further machines.

Opposite page
Scizor from
Pokémon

This page
Pikachu and Ash
from *Pokémon*

This page
Pong
screenshot

Opposite page
Breakout
screenshot

The following year, the world's second commercial videogame, *Pong*, was released by Atari, and players enjoyed it the world over. In the mid '70s, just as the advanced version of *Pong*, *Breakout* (Atari), was gaining popularity, Japanese developers began designing games (mostly copies of *Breakout*), and videogames were soon to be found in bars and games arcades. Among these, *Space Invaders*, by Taito, became a social phenomenon on such a scale that it will probably never be paralleled. The game design was essentially a variation of *Breakout*. The rather abstract blocks became 'invaders', which were made to advance threateningly towards the player. *Space Invaders* became a big hit in the autumn of 1978, and it seemed that not only the games arcades, but nearly every coffee shop in Japan was equipped with a machine. This all happened just as the Japanese economy was gearing up to the economic boom of the 1980s, while the American economy was beginning to decline in the aftermath of the Vietnam War and the oil crisis. The game was so popular that it created a scare over the shortage of 100-yen coins. Among the young die-hard fans of *Space Invaders* was Satoshi Tajiri, the future creator of *Pokémon*. He has said that the origins of *Pokémon* lie in bug collecting, which fascinated him as a child, and in these 'invaders' which he encountered when he was 13.

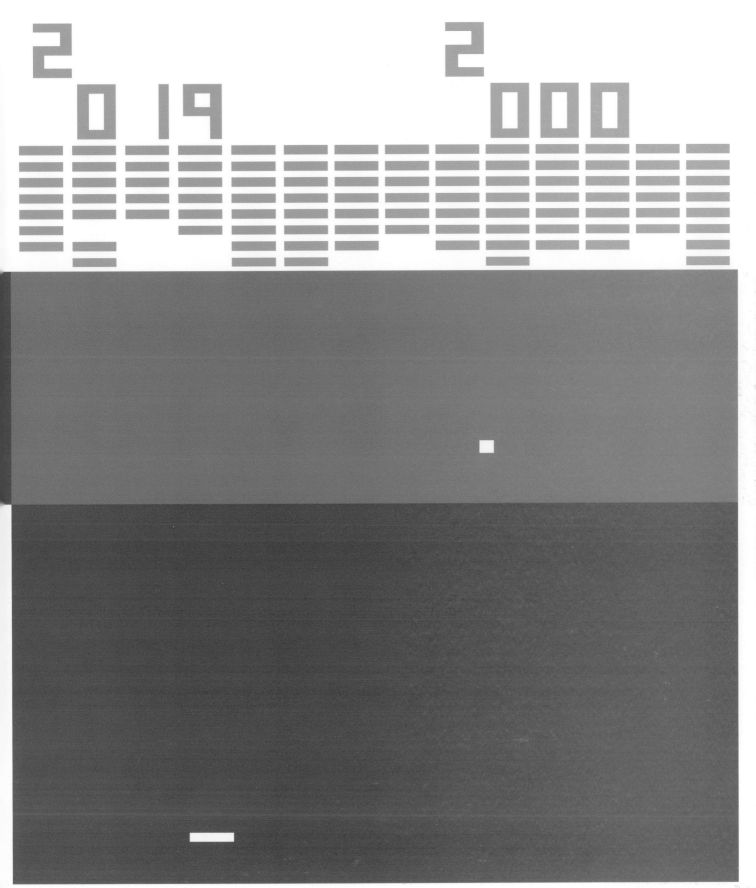

This page top
Disco Space Invaders
by Funny Stuff,
1978

This page bottom
An *Invader House*
Coffee Shop, 1978

Opposite page
Game Boy

From that time on, Tajiri became absolutely engrossed in videogames. Not only did he play, but he began teaching himself to become a designer, so that he could eventually become part of the creative process of that which he enjoyed so much. Such aspirations were in no way dissimilar from the goals of many a teenage rock-music fan or comic collector. What set Tajiri apart, however, was his journalistic fervour – he printed his own game strategy guide.

In 1983, when Tajiri was 18, Namco released *Xevious*. The game was a revelation for him. It was a vertically scrolling shooter, a highly evolved version of *Space Invaders*. Tajiri became a devoted player, and he created a new magazine called *Indies*, which belonged to the still-new genre of 'game strategy mini-comics'. Tajiri wrote the magazine himself, ran off copies, stapled them by hand, and took them to bookstores, or sent them by mail (online sales were not yet an option).

The strategy guide garnered attention alongside *Xevious* itself, which was rising in popularity, and Tajiri began a professional career writing a column on arcade games in a popular Japanese videogame magazine. From the beginning, Tajiri had a clear goal of becoming a games designer, and so while continuing his work as a writer, he began developing games at *Indies* with his college-student friends.

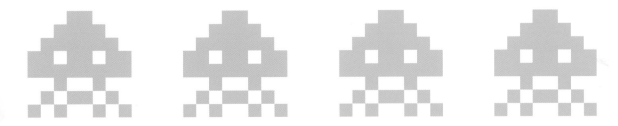

Six years after *Xevious*, their endeavours bore fruit. *Quinty* was released in 1989 by Namco on the Famicom platform. The success of this game allowed Tajiri to create a new company, Game Freak. This was also the year Nintendo released the Game Boy. As soon as Tajiri saw the Game Boy's 'communication cable', he began conceptualizing *Pokémon*. At Game Freak, the design code for *Pokémon* was #002, next in line after *Quinty*. The game took six years to make, starting in 1990.

Different games achieved different levels of popularity inside and outside Japan. The biggest global hit of the 1980s was most certainly Namco's *Pac-Man* (1980). *Pac-Man* was, of course, a hit in Japan as well, and *Space Invaders* was a hit overseas. But in Japan, the two games that influenced Tajiri, *Space Invaders* and *Xevious*, became cultural sensations on a scale comparable with rock music.

Part of Tajiri's idea for trading monsters in *Pokémon* came from his experience with the Japanese role-playing game (RPG) *Dragon Quest*. He tells us that when players found unusual items, they often wished they could trade them with their friends.

Dragon Quest was a best-seller in Japan, shifting millions of copies, but outside Japan, it has attracted little attention. Thus, the three games that influenced Tajiri's creation of *Pokémon* were only huge hits in Japan.

Pokémon is a standard RPG, but it also has the unique feature of allowing players to trade monsters through the use of a cable connecting game machines. When the Game Boy was first released, *Tetris* was a global hit, and Game Boys were connected to allow real-time battles. However, Tajiri noticed that the name for the cable was not 'battle' but 'communication' cable. *Pokémon* allowed more than metaphorical communication; it made use of a system that created actual communication – a network game. The incredible success of *Pokémon* happened to coincide with the rapid spread of Internet usage in Japan, but its communication system differed from games that had come before it and even from the Internet itself.

After the web browser, the Internet device that had the greatest worldwide impact was the music-trading software Napster, which came onto the scene in 1999. Users connected to the Napster server could share music files they had saved on their hard drives with other users at no charge. This was different from CD rental. When a track was saved onto a new PC, it stayed in the hard drive, ready to be downloaded by the next user. It was like a water-bucket relay, only with some water staying in the hands of each person in the chain. This method of transfer is generally referred to as 'peer-to-peer' (P2P) communication.'

This page left

Pong
arcade cabinet

This page right

Space Invaders
arcade cabinet

Opposite page top

Tetris
screenshot

**Opposite page
centre**

Dragon Quest
screenshot

**Opposite page
bottom**

Pac-Man
screenshot

In the case of a *Pokémon* exchange, the peer with whom you trade data is a real, live human being standing in front of you with a game machine in hand. The cables link the two machines, and the data is transferred from one machine to the other, in a primitive form of P2P communication. However, there is a crucial difference with the Napster method. In the case of *Pokémon*, the data is not copied from machine A to machine B but is rather 'cut and pasted'. In this metaphorical relay, the water (or data) is lost once it is passed on.

One of the goals for a *Pokémon* player is the completion of the *Monster Encyclopedia*, which requires the collection of every last character in the game. Preserving the rarity of characters within the game is crucial to this. The uncommonness of certain monsters excites interest in the player, extending the duration and enjoyment of the game, and encouraging a new type of peer-to-peer communication among players. The game's producer, Ishihara Tsunekazu, describes this marvellously designed communication model as 'not-closed':

'The most significant aspect of the *Pokémon* concept is the fact that it is a "not-closed" product. Take film: we see a beginning, an end, and finally, the credits rolling. That is a "closed" product. The Game Boy title *Pokémon* also has a beginning and an end, and even credits. But for the player, this hardly means that the game is over. After the end, in order to complete the *Monster Encyclopedia*, the player sets out once again for the towns and forests in search of *Pokémon*. Also, a player may use the cable to trade *Pokémon* with other players, and can find new and more evolved *Pokémon*. In the process, the player makes a whole circle of "communication friends".

Videogames that came before *Pokémon* had never entailed such a laborious process. In fact, one of the pluses of videogames was the very fact that you could enjoy them without any interpersonal communication. But when we set out to make hand-held videogames into communication tools, the software itself could no longer be "closed".' (*Intercommunication*, July 2000)

The 'not-closed' communication model of both the game and cards is the single largest reason why *Pokémon* became such a mega-hit worldwide. The fact that the designers refrained from using the word 'open' suggests that it is fundamentally different from the 'open system' of the Internet.

Opposite page

Ash and Pikachu
from *Pokémon*

I do not intend to suggest that this communication model is inherently Japanese. However, there is a connection between the three games mentioned that influenced Tajiri and the 'not-closed' system. *Space Invaders* and *Xevious* can both be enjoyed on three different levels. Firstly, they can be played as ordinary games. Secondly, there are game secrets. In *Space Invaders*, the score for shooting invaders changed depending upon the number of shots used (from our present perspective, a primitive secret indeed – and yet the designers were sure that it would not be discovered!). In *Xevious*, a hidden character was intentionally designed into the game. When the player shot in a certain pattern, one that bore no relation to the game itself, a hidden 'flag' appeared, and the player received an extra fighter ship.

Thirdly, players can search for bugs. They revel in making the game behave in ways that were not intended by the designers, and the knowledge of such bugs spreads within the community. This happened with both these games. These three levels of play include aspects that are 'not-closed', as well as, in fact, 'not intended'.

Recall the rare items in *Dragon Quest*. The die-hard players will continue playing even after the story has ended in order to find such items. Recent RPGs are specially designed so that players do not easily lose interest, but in the rudimentary RPGs of the 1980s, there was plenty of fun to be had in the search for rare items. These games were in a sense 'un-closed', but were also too tight to allow cross-communication.

Spacer Invaders, *Xevious* and *Dragon Quest* all present some aspects of the 'not-closed' concept of *Pokémon*. And all three were huge hits in Japan.

Perhaps the striking worldwide success of *Pokémon* should not be considered the result of the adoption of 'Japanese culture' on a global level (as with sushi), but should be seen as two cultures meeting halfway in the 1990s, as Japan became more Westernized and the West became more open to foreign culture. Gone are the days when, in the realm of entertainment, globalization meant only Americanization.

Masuyama

ALL CLICKED OUT

    (1)   PLAY   (2)

0000   0000   0000

MAZZI BINAISA

SCORE<1>   HI-S ORE   SCORE<2>

0000   2600   0000

3   CREDIT 00

My hate-hate relationship with videogames started on Christmas Day 1981 at 11.30 in the morning. I remember the time clearly, not particularly for what Father Christmas was kind enough to leave me, but for the red-and-white striped box that revolutionized the life of my 11-year-old brother and millions of kids worldwide. He leapt, jumped and thanked everyone and promptly fell silent as he worked out how to play the game.

As he became more proficient, my young mind was struck by how anti-social *Space Invaders* was. The screen was small, allowing for only one small head and its accompanying field of vision to enjoy it at a time. Added to this were the simplistic graphics, with their incessant rows of green bugs – sorry, aliens – ready to get the player. Of course, it was this design feature that gave *Space Invaders* its hypnotic, somewhat addictive quality. Unlike a book, you did not have to use your imagination to visualize the characters, and the joystick gave my brother the impression that he was somehow active when in fact he was pacified. It's a concept that game designers have been modifying ever since. For the remainder of the Christmas break, I had a shadow sibling who was always distracted unless he was settled in a chair with his black plastic cuboid.

Of course videogames, rather like music, are a social barometer of our times. It wasn't long before *Space Invaders* was so last season and was replaced by *Pac-Man*. *Pac-Man* embodies the decade in which he emerged. Like Gordon Gekko in *Wall Street* he believed that greed was good. *Pac-Man* was hot on the playground as he was the perfect accompaniment to the consumerist times. There seemed to be no point to his quest other than to be chased by ghosts, yet his fans were numerous. To my pseudo-intellectual pre-teen head, loathe as I then was to admit it, the games craze spelt the guaranteed mental atrophy of my contemporaries. How could something with such a facile premise hook so many, so completely? But looked at in a wider context, videogames offered the participants instant gratification. They begged no questions for those who were really into them. Instead, they provided an imagined community, one that I witnessed many times in the clusters of teenagers hanging out in arcades as they desperately tried to immortalize themselves on leader boards.

Opposite page top

Sonic the Hedgehog

Opposite page bottom

Space Invaders

This page

Street Fighter 3 Third Strike

Perhaps my most sophisticated computer-generated nemesis was *Sonic*. Unlike their predecessors, *Sonic* on the Sega system and its rival *Super Mario Bros* on Nintendo, leant themselves to multi-players. *Sonic* was also very cool. The little blue hedgehog's popularity tied in with the dance music craze as he pirouetted in the sky, gobbling up magic rings. Unlike *Pac-Man* he did not grow fat but developed an ability to jump implausibly high from platforms. In short, *Sonic* was a mirror image of the drug-taking, dance-all-night crew that played him. Sonic's expression even changed into a mini-frown when he 'scored', and just like the scary 17-year-old who mixed speed, ketamine and a vodka chaser there was no stopping him. *Sonic* became the game of choice before driving around for 45 minutes looking for a warehouse party. The multi-player feature also allowed gameheads to think that they were being social as it was often played in teams. It was then that my dislike of videogames was compounded, as during one late-night session my hand-eye co-ordination was shown to be no better on a keypad than in PE. I felt conned: if everyone else found it so easy, did it mean that I was some kind of freak? Again I hoped that, as with *Sonic*'s predecessors, everyone would get bored and move on to something else.

They did – to the über-violent and terribly slick. *Street Fighter* and *Mortal Kombat* were the precursors to the gut-wrenching *Unreal Tournament* and *Quake*. Whereas with games of the *Street Fighter* ilk, I could chuckle at the implausibly high kicks of Chun Li as she took out a giant Sumo wrestler, with *Unreal* and *Quake* I can now only look away. Their constituency seems to be almost exclusively guys my age. Multi-play is an option, but invariably individuals play against each other, the objective being to beat the life out of one another. The demise of each contestant is always grisly. It is not surprising that these games appeal to the said demographic. Unlike their fathers, these men did not grow up with the spectre of global war over them.

In tracking the evolution of the videogame, I realize that it is not to blame for any dumbing-down of the youth. The games that people play are a reflection of their wants and also of our growing desire as a society to be preoccupied. Videogames are escapist, they do not challenge us in the way that many traditional games do. Yes, some require strategy, but agility on a keypad is a great leveller. Where word of email has superseded word of mouth, it is perhaps not surprising that 'Old Entertainment', rather like the Old Economy, has been cast aside. But I remain hopeful, not just because the general public are clocking onto the repetitive strain injury that is theirs for the taking, but also because in many ways the surprise factor in playing games has faded over the last 20 years. They are no longer a luxury item, or indeed the new cool. For millions globally they will simply be a footnote of their youth.

Mazzi Binaisa

ANDREAS LANGE EUROPEAN GAMES CULTURE

It is an exciting period
for the European gaming
scene. Something
is happening in every
corner of the continent.

The new games console is the star of the exhibition. Huge numbers of people crowd into the pavilion to be able at least to catch a glimpse of the global innovation. The excitement is so intense that the police have to restore order again and again. Following its debut in London, the games console causes great commotion in Berlin as well. Even the Minister for Trade and Commerce is not prepared to miss this opportunity and dares to have a little go. But hang on a minute. Games consoles? A debut in London? The Minister for Trade and Commerce? What sounds like a distant, futuristic fantasy is actually a real event – but one from the dim and distant past.

The year was 1951. The world was experiencing the première of the first genuine games computer, called Nimrod, after the man who built the Tower of Babel. The British company Ferranti had just produced the first commercial computer – the Ferranti Mark 1 – in co-operation with the University of Manchester. Now all that remained was to sell it. The idea was captivating: Ferranti developed a genuine games computer on the basis of the Mark 1 and presented it to the astonished masses at trade exhibitions in London and Berlin. Thousands of visitors competed against it. They played Nim, a simple strategy game involving 16 matches. Although Nim could be played on an accounting robot produced by the American company Westinghouse as early as 1939 at the World Exhibition in New York, Nimrod can justifiably claim the title of the world's first games computer. For the first time, a games console worked entirely electronically, that is to say, like a real computer. For a brief period Europe was ahead in the field of interactive digital entertainment.

But obviously nobody was aware of the implications of this invention at the time. Following the Berlin show, Nimrod was broken down again into its constituent parts and forgotten. Its disassembly is symbolic of how difficult it was for entertainment software in Europe to be recognized as culturally and economically interesting. Europeans only slowly began to understand that digital games had a not inconsiderable share in the path to the information society and would continue to do so in the future – quite apart from the fact that one can make good money from them.

Writing about games and Europe, one is not reporting from the epicentre of the global games scene. The tempo is set by the USA and Japan. The consumer is always made painfully aware of this whenever a new videogame system is launched. Generally it does not arrive in European shops until after its release in Japan and the USA – often at a higher price.

Opposite page
Nimrod Computer
1951

Despite this, Europe plays a significant part in the international games business. This is connected on the one hand to European purchasing power. Of the estimated $17.7 billion global market for computer and videogames in 2000, Europe, at $5.8 billion, ranked ahead of Japan ($3.4 billion) and only just behind the USA ($6.3 billion) (Figures: Chart Track/CTW). Its ability to manufacture internationally popular games is also long-established. *Tomb Raider* wasn't the first game made in Europe to become an international success. *Populous*, the first game by possibly the best-known European developer, the Englishman Peter Molyneux, was a worldwide hit as early as 1989, with some four million copies sold. It also established the new genre of god games.

But can one speak of Europe at all in this connection? Is there such a thing as a European view? Or is a common television standard the only thing linking European countries? (In contrast to Japan and the USA, the PAL television standard has become established in Europe. Videogames must be modified to adapt them to the respective television standard.) In fact, Europe is very heterogeneous, and traditionally characterized in the games business by the three major West European countries where games are produced and consumed, the United Kingdom, Germany and France. During the Cold War, a games scene could scarcely become established behind the Iron Curtain because there was hardly any dissemination of home computers or videogames. Only now are Eastern European and smaller Western European countries becoming the focus of attention as developers and producers of internationally successful games. (The best known exception is *Tetris* which is reputed to be the most played game of all time worldwide. It is ironic that the most successful European videogame was programmed in 1984 in Russia, a country otherwise so insignificant for games.)

The space available means this survey has to concentrate on the three countries mentioned above. However, even there games are produced and sold under very different conditions. All European countries have one thing in common: computer and videogames first arrived in the shops as imports. The games industry was born in the USA at the beginning of the 1970s. The typical American mixture of entrepreneurial spirit and enthusiasm for technical innovation provided the right breeding ground for it. US citizens also have far fewer reservations than Europeans about unadulterated entertainment. When the videogame market, which was dominated by America, collapsed almost overnight in mid-1984, it was Japanese companies that exploited the opportunity and laid the foundation stone for their current dominance in this sector. The Europeans shared the American view that the videogame boom of the early years was finally at an end. A misjudgment, as we know today.

One of the reasons for the videogame crash was the arrival of playable and affordable home computers such as the Commodore 64 at the beginning of the 1980s. These enjoyed great popularity in Europe, among younger members of the public in particular. Anybody who wanted to could now program his or her own games. In the UK, above all, programming games developed on a large scale as a hobby. This was not a matter of chance. The UK was the only European country in which the successful production of home computers developed at the time. Companies such as Sinclair, Acorn and Amstrad made a substantial contribution to the popularization of the home computer at the beginning of the decade. Sinclair's ZX80 and ZX81, which appeared in 1980 and 1981, were conceived as didactic computers. With a price tag of under £100, they were no more expensive than a games console. The Sinclair ZX Spectrum, which appeared in 1982, became a smash hit because of its suitability for games. It was also responsible for the success of the first British/European computer game star. *Dizzy*, which was invented in 1986 by Oliver Twins (18 years old at the time), was the most played series on the Spectrum. In 1993 Philip and Andrew Oliver founded Blitz Games, now one of the most important games developers in Britain.

The BBC Computer Literacy Project, which started in 1981, not only promoted British people's understanding of the opportunities provided by the new microcomputers with numerous broadcasts but also launched its own computer, the BBC Micro, onto the market. More than one million of these computers (produced by Acorn) have been sold since 1982.

Since no comparable production developed in other European countries, microcomputers and consequently games production were given far less support. In Germany, for example, there were just as many young people writing their own games for fun, but they were perceived more as a type of subculture than as the possible nucleus of a future growth market. A further starting advantage for English developers lay in their common language and relative cultural proximity to the home of digital, interactive entertainment. It was far easier for them than for the rest of Europe to get into business with established American developers and publishers and consequently to obtain finance. By contrast, in France, with its sense of national pride, cultural differences with America may well have been a reason for the emergence of a robust home-grown games industry. If, as in France, a quota of national cultural production in the traditional media is prescribed by law, it will scarcely be acceptable for foreign productions to dominate the interactive media sector. In recent years, French companies such as Infogrames, Ubi Soft or Titus have evolved into internationally important players through takeovers of European and American companies.

Opposite page top
Sinclair ZX81

Opposite page bottom
Sinclair ZX Spectrum

This page top
Dizzy screenshot

This page bottom
Dizzy

In Germany, however, the games industry led a Cinderella-like existence for a long time. From the mid-1980s, the first money from computer games came mainly from custom-made German adaptations of American games. Thus, independent production of specifically German games emerged comparatively slowly. German teams of developers such as Blue Byte (*Battle Isle/The Setters*) remained the exception. This did not change until the mid-1990s with the emergence of the Neuer Markt. With fresh capital from the stock exchange, it was now possible to build up larger structures. Phenomedia AG, which was founded in 1999 and which created Germany's most popular videogame character Moorhuhn, is a good example. This series emerged from a free advertising game. Though the first two versions were downloaded more than 24 million times free of charge from the Internet, more than 600,000 copies of the PC, PlayStation and Game Boy versions were sold. This is a clear indicator that games in Germany have now expanded out of the relatively narrow confines of hardcore game players.

Computer games are bearers of cultural values and traditions. It is not surprising, therefore, that different types of games are successful in different cultural circles. Europe has always been closer to the USA than to Japan because of common cultural roots. So there have only been exceptional cases of American or European games being hits in Japan. Conversely, however, it is entirely normal for Japanese games to occupy the top slots in Western charts. One of the reasons why the West had difficulty getting a foothold in the Japanese market is that in Japan PCs play virtually no role as games platforms. Another reason lies in the type of games preferred. While role-playing games in particular enjoy great popularity in Japan, in the West it is action, strategy and sports games that are regularly found in the charts. Japanese games were also closely linked with the anime and manga pop culture. But Europeans have so far remained largely untouched by this culture.

But even within Europe different mentalities have shaped different types of games. France, where comic strips have a long and significant tradition, distinguished itself with graphically outstanding adventures and multimedia productions. At the important French entertainment software trade fair held in Cannes, the Milia, computer games are always found alongside a range of other media and information carriers. The important role played by the French media giant Vivendi in the French games scene is an indicator of the fact that the French do not see computer games as a separate, isolated field of endeavour, but as a natural part of their national culture and media industry.

In England, by contrast, a self-confident games industry developed early (from 1982). This found its expression in the establishment of the ECTS in London, Europe's first games fair aimed at a specialist public. With regard to games content, the English, like the Americans, love action games. This is why videogame consoles suitable for action games are more widespread in England than in other European countries.

Germany, on the other hand, has one of the most distinctive PC games markets worldwide. Apparently German players were better prepared than others to face the configuration problems that previously arose in running a game on a PC ('which port is used by my sound card?'). This enjoyment of matters technical also distinguished German productions for a long time. Developers liked to concentrate on the quality of programming technology. In so doing, they sometimes lost sight of playing the game, which is why German programmers had difficulty finding international publishers. Enjoyment of handicrafts may also be responsible for the Germans' preference for complex construction-strategy games like *Anno 1602*. The German-Austrian coproduction by the Sunflowers company rates as the top-selling computer game of all time in Germany, with more than one million copies sold in German-speaking countries alone.

It is an exciting period for the European gaming scene. Something is happening in every corner of the continent. Games such as *Max Payne™* from Finland (Remedy), *Commandos* from Spain (Pyro) and *Hidden and Dangerous* from the Czech Republic (Illusion Softworks) show that internationally successful games can now be developed in every European country. The Austrian company Jowood is a good example of how producers from previously less important countries are now also to be reckoned with in the publishing sector.

The next generation of consoles as well as the further development of PCs as a multimedia platform have led to a deeper penetration of private households. The European market is therefore now of a size to make it easier for European companies to generate enough capital to expand its production and sales capacity further. This greater self-confidence is also expressed in new events such as the computer and videogames trade fair, the Games Convention planned for autumn 2002 in Leipzig, and the establishment of the first European association representing the interests of independent games developers (TIGA) in 2001.

The UK – always a hair's breadth ahead of other European countries where cultural exports are concerned – included entertainment software in its Creative Industries Programme, which started in 1997. Since then the export and production of British games has been supported to the same extent as British music and films. But games are not only being increasingly recognized as an economic factor. As director of the Berlin Computer Games Museum, which was opened in distinctly modest circumstances in 1997, I am particularly pleased that established cultural institutions such as the Barbican Centre in London have also discovered what an exciting cultural phenomenon games can be.

Even in the field of training, which still represents one of the greatest problems for European videogame production, there appears to be movement. At the beginning of 2001, the University of Abertay Dundee opened an institute especially for the promotion and further development of entertainment software in Scotland with the IC CAVE (International Centre for Computer Games and Virtual Entertainment). The fact that this institution is supported by, among others, the European Community's European Regional Development Fund is a good sign. It shows that a growing awareness of the significance of entertainment software may be brought about by the process of European unification.

However, it is still difficult for the European industries to find a strong common voice. Different languages constitute a considerable barrier. Moreover, the cultural sector, in particular, varies largely between nations. While guidelines (e.g. for copyright law) have been drawn up at EU level, it is up to each individual country to implement the recommendations in national law within this frequently large range of variants. It will therefore be some time, for example, before Europe has standard regulations for the protection of young people.

Even if the cultural diversity causes problems with regard to global competitiveness, this should not be viewed as negative, but as a source of creativity. However, cultural production can only thrive where there are good conditions for growth. Understanding that the common cultural inheritance of Europe is reflected just as much in digital game stories as in so-called 'high' culture, would be a crucial first step. The promotion of training and talent and consequently the development of the interactive entertainment culture would follow. This is a common spiritual basis on which all those interested in an active, formative role for Europe in the information age can meet – including, of course, those who simply want to play good games.

Andreas Lange

Opposite page left
Max Payne™

Opposite page centre
*Hidden and
Dangerous 2*

Opposite page right
*Hidden and
Dangerous 2*

This page
Max Payne™

Acknowledgements:
I should like to express my heart-felt
thanks to the following people. Their
profound knowledge of the European
games scene has made a significant
contribution to the creation of
this essay: Nigel Davis, Manager of
The Independent Games Developer
Association (TIGA), Manager (Blitz
Games); Alexander Jorias, Developer
(Massive Development), Organizer
Unterhaltungssoftware (Entertainment
Software) Forum (USF); Jacqui Lyon,
Computer Game Agent (Marjacq);
Ronald Schaefer, Managing Director
Verband der Unterhaltungssoftware
Deutschlands (VUD: Association
of German Entertainment Software);
Teut Weidemann, Developer and
Managing Director (Wings Simulations).

*MY STORY: GIRLS PLAYING GAMES *

```
   (1)      PLAY        (2)
 0000      0000       0000
```

ALICE TAYLOR

Thought: Ever (*ever*) Seen a Videogame Advertised in Female-Oriented Media?

I always did like fighting with boys. They were always the interesting-looking lot – muddy, messy and making noise. I read the *Beano* and *Dandy* and Willard Price and Nancy Drew. I had my light sabre and plastic R2D2 aged six, football skillz badges aged eight, needlework and recorder aged nine. Light sabre versus the recorder? Football versus needlework? Am I really that odd as a game-playing girl?

I have lived though the evolution of videogames, sampling them as I went along. I recall these events with a fondness that's hard to describe. My first look-in was simple: I was nine years old, visiting a playmate, and there it was – a brand new ZX81. The latest in educational tools! Best of all, it plugged into the television. Magic. Tellies weren't supposed to do anything but show *Dr Who* and *Blake 7* episodes, of course, although unfortunately such perfect entertainment was insistently interrupted by *Newsround* and wildlife programmes. But plug in this magic box and yes-s-s, something to fight over until Tom Baker was back on. Stuff on the telly that you control, wow, this was new shit, and we knew it. This was cool.

Secondary school. I was 12 now, and there was the computer room, humming quietly with acres of beige and black plastic and big fat keyboards: an idling herd of BBC Micros, inviting pouncing. The computer teacher was, with hindsight, patently a gamer: in exchange for learning a line or two of BASIC, we'd be allowed to play *Frogger* and *Sphinx Adventure* for hours. It was an all-girls school, and the room would be overflowing at lunchtime, beeping and rocking. Those ladies are all out there somewhere today.

Then came my powered-down years. Aged 15, smoking, drinking and makeup were much more fun than the aging Micro. Travelling, clothes, London, clubbing – I don't think I saw a videogame for maybe six or seven years, beyond the odd foray on an Atari Jaguar and a couple of coin-ops here and there. I didn't consciously miss electronic gaming – remember how busy you were as a teenager? But when I returned to them – or rather they to me – it was like an old friend coming home: it was 1993, I was 22, and Dad had bought a Game Boy.

Dad was cool like that. Dad taught me and sis pool, and took us to the pub with him as kids. He'd get his pint and crisps, and ask for the change in 2ps, to keep us quiet on the *Donkey Kong Junior* in the pub hallway. Was I the only girl to play *Space Invaders* after going swimming, using the change left over after you got your crisps out of the vending machine? Surely not. So, my dad flips me this grey box thing, the *Tetris* cart already in place. Look what I got! he says, excitedly, what do you think? He didn't see it again.

I think that's where the blur started. *Zelda* on the Game Boy was with me for about four months, tucked into my jeans pocket. My daily Tube journey ripped by in seconds. Someone gave me their Mega Drive – *Sonic*, my cheeky little hero, I still adore you. *Road Rash*: my best mate, Corinna, and I – a controller each, a glass of wine, an open fire, hook-chaining and giggling into the night. 1995. PlayStation. Lara! Jesus, look at her legs, isn't she fab? Corinna would do the spotting and pointing and I'd do the controlling, and the pre-pub hours would tick by. We'd play the entire game like that, managing to make a single-player adventure game into a giggly girls' night in. The same with *Resident Evil*, the pair of us screaming at all the scary bits with gleeful joy.

PC CD-ROM

Opposite page

Zelda
from Game Boy

This page

*Frogger 2:
Swampy's
Revenge*

1996. *Quake*. Oh God, what is this? This was trouble. When the after-work pub session was over, I'd end up back in the office, fragging away until the early hours, completely addicted. Say no more, I still play it – you'll find me on #ctfpickup on gamesnet, defending flags on a daily basis. I nearly got the *Quake* Q tattooed somewhere…
I only didn't because I couldn't decide where. I bought a PC, ostensibly for work, blatantly for gaming. The N64 arrived – so beautiful! – I grabbed one immediately, gagging for some *Mario Kart* and the next incarnation of *Zelda*. The Dreamcast just for *Soul Calibur* and *Code Veronica*. And on it goes.

But why do you play so many games, Alice? Do I, I think? Yeah, I suppose I do, especially (as most people point out) compared to other females. Why? It's fun. It's social, and entertaining, and interesting, and unpredictable. I don't watch much television, I get bored with it in the main. Hell isn't other people – it's being made to watch *EastEnders*.

So where to from here? I'll play games for the rest of my life, that much is obvious. I also believe there are many, many other women out there who have shared my history, at least in part. There's a line that is consistently quoted by journalists to start a piece: 'Games are second only to Hollywood, and bigger than music' or some such. Well, get this – off the top of my head, videogames are the only thing on this planet except Grecian 2000 that are only marketed towards men. You think it's big now, wait a while. When women stop being told that games are only for sweaty young males, there will be a minor revolution.

I'll finish with an aside. When the famous PlayStation adverts were released, in a blaze of androgynous, pierced, sexy glory, I thought, rocking. There we go. For once, there was merchandise too – T-shirts and the like, carrying the sexy symbols of this new kit. About time too, I thought, there never was a *Quake* babydoll shirt (a regret of mine still), but I'll get a PlayStation one, preferably with just the symbols across the front, and in plain black. Something cute. What did they print? A black babydoll, yes… but with 'PLAYSTATION WIDOW' printed on it.

I didn't buy one.

Alice Taylor

*BROADS A BITCH NEVER THE SNITCH:
MY LIFE AND VIDEO GAMES

```
     (1)      PLAY        (2)
   0000      0000       0000
*JEREMY RELPH*
```

Videogames run through my life like the music I listen to. They provide marker points for memories, pleasant and otherwise. But videogames aren't anything other than what they are: they just are.

Her name is Kelly* and she liked to drink vodka all day like she lived in a Belle and Sebastian song. Before she crawled her intelligent (bona-fide genius), slim ass into the bottle (or wineskin) she was my world as I watched her master level after level of *Mario Brothers* in her mother's nicotine-stained townhouse. When she was done she'd smoke a cigarette and fuck with my face, pulling it in different directions like I was Jim Carrey, talking about how malleable it was. I don't miss those days. It was grade ten and I was trying to be a roughneck like the NWA and assorted hardcore shit I was listening to, but I was soft like the Depeche Mode torch songs I despised.

I never got the timing down with *Mario Brothers*, and never got the timing down to enjoy a normal, calm relationship. The drama quotient was high, and I always left Kelly's place feeling like a neutered jackass, with my heart racing like the stupid soundtrack to that stupid game, a feeling numbed only by chain-smoking, hash and the huffing of hair mousse.

I, of course, never had my own Nintendo system, so I was destined to get schooled every time I tried to hang with the people who spent all their waking moments tearing up level after level with li'l Mario and Luigi. I grabbed some space on the grimy carpet, hid behind a wall of smoke, compliments of my Dunhills and talked smack to the rest of the family, never mentioning of course that Mario and Luigi were negative and damaging depictions of Italians as short, fat labourers – or skilled craftsmen if you like to put a positive spin on things – no, I was above such obvious, insecurity-inspired remarks.

'Winners Don't Use Drugs.' That used to be an advertisement from the US government which appeared at the beginning of arcade games, something my boys and I found laughable as we clocked high scores and honeys. I'm a winner, no? I see these sober kids struggling in *Super Sprint* and my stoned ass is playing for keeps? Do the math on that, Poindexter. Keep it clean like Young MC, bust a corny move and I'll win every time. Too bad the same rules of conduct didn't apply to life: get stoned and win! Winners get zooted!

Too many stupid little bad things happened at these convenience stores, from continuous minor theft competitions to showdowns with the cops – being accused of being gang members (cops in the suburbs have to amuse themselves, I suppose), having my brand-new Ricky Barnes skateboard stolen and being too fried to mention it to the cops who rolled by. Back then, the only things that had any real value were quarters and foil-wrapped dimes of herb.

Somewhere along the line my drug use caught up with me and kicked my ass into a serious depression. I couldn't stop drinking and getting fucked up, yet felt no relief from loneliness in my constant inebriation: that game just stopped working. No amount of dimes or quarters or distractions worked.

And I ended up in rehab in the wonderful city of Minneapolis. Happy to be smoking American cigarettes, I decided to give sobriety a kick. And it started to work. I, however, still had my own ideas about what living clean was about, so when my roommate at a halfway house snuck in at three in the morning with a drunken buzz and stolen goods, I didn't say boo.

The halfway house bought me some time away from the temptations of home. It was peopled with addicts like myself, most with far more impressive stories of self-destruction than mine. Situated in a former hotel beside a highway, it was full of smoke, coffee and people struggling to go against their self-destructive natures. From tracksuited Tony the former mob-affiliated bookie, who managed to smoke three packs of Marlboro Reds a day and who became my defender due to my wise-ass big mouth, to the recovering coke-freak musician Angela who'd made it onto COPS and regaled me with stories of anal sex and enemas, there were some characters there.

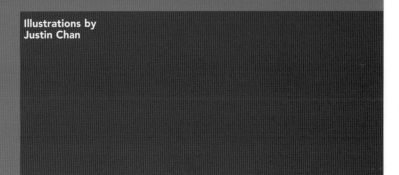

Illustrations by
Justin Chan

It was three months of growth and limbo. I spent my days chain-smoking and blowing O's at the ceiling wondering what I was doing in Minneapolis. And just trying to stop wondering, period.

Now, the way this halfway house worked was, you follow the rules or you're out. The rules were simple: get a job, follow curfew, attend meetings, don't sleep with anyone and don't drink or do drugs or you're out. Oh, and report anyone who breaks any of the above rules. It sounded corny, trite and juvenile, but it made sense. After all, quitting a lifestyle meant quitting a lifestyle and replacing it with something perhaps a little less destructive.

My second roommate, Steve, had different plans. His were: don't do crystal meth, but drink and smoke herb and break into shit.

When he stumbled in one night with his boy Rico at three in the morning, my conscience was kicking. So I went back to sleep. Waking up, I was mad nervous. Do I rat, or say nothing and risk getting kicked out? I wasn't looking to get kicked for anything other than fucking up and breaking to the calls of the dealers on Minneapolis's main strip. I might have been lazy and surly, but I certainly wasn't no rat. He slumbered with the scent of booze in the air, a previously empty corner of the room filled with the spoils of the big heist: a big airbrush machine, a small TV and, God bless him, a Super Nintendo System.

Playing *NHLPA* all day made my decision simple: he'd fuck up and get his own ass kicked out, and I could enjoy videogames galore until that day.

The first time I saw *NHLPA* on a borrowed PlayStation 2 I nearly lost my shit. I immediately knew that my time was no longer my own. My time belonged to the PS2, until someone came and got it.

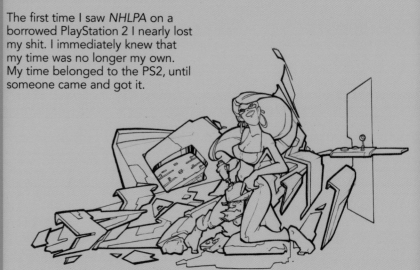

Funny, because the first time I saw Therese, a well-bootied honey, my heart skipped crazily. I just looked at her, the way she moved and it was just like dying. She was mad sexy in her slightly elevated boots, tight jeans accentuating her bubble butt, tight yellow T-shirt and cornrows. The way she walked right past me like I wasn't even there, like I was a wall or some shit, it killed me. I knew right at that moment that I had to have it (the booty, that is).

Around that time I found myself single. My long-term girlfriend had dropped me after returning from a work term in Ecuador, trading up for some Ecuadorian cat (the kind she swore she despised, which had always made me nervous).

Illustrations by Justin Chan

After that relationship, I learned something. Like a wisened Sade, I had a bulletproof soul. More to the point, I felt like Pac-Man. I'd eaten a power pellet and felt indestructible. I could run through any scenario with a honey and come out unaffected. Which was a nice way of avoiding unpleasant feelings.

Which brings me back to the booty-blessed honey, she of the cornrows. I ran smooth game on her while on break at a mall where I was working for a couple of weeks. She worked at the flower shop, where I coincidentally bought my grandmother some 'Get Well Soon' flowers. Mad bonus points for that. With my super *Pac-Man* force I ran game on her with the quickness, with her co-worker to bear witness to my diabolical quick wit. I was slick, things just clicked. Discussing my grandmother's recovering health (it helps to play honestly), I segued smoothly to a request for her digits. Her eyes narrowed, suspecting something was afoot. She parried with 'And when will you call me?'. Cool player that I was, knowing that I was most certainly in it to hit it, I deftly responded 'Sometime. Whenever.' This did not meet with her approval. I slithered off, checking her fine features and offhandedly remarked 'A'ight. I'mma have to go back to the lab and see what I can concoct. I'll check you Monday then.'

Five minutes later, back at work, her co-worker dropped me a card with a playfully threatening note. And her digits.

Needless to say, I got mine, had some good times and learned this simple truth: if it's booty you want, booty you'll get. Any man can score some ass. I, however, was too wrapped up in my *Pac-Man* metaphor. Replaying my suave responses to her not-so-subtle overtures of love, I marvelled at my own cold-heartedness. She'd run at me like one of those ghosts saying, 'You're so sexy, you're so kind, you smell so dope, I really like you', and I'd counter with 'You're mad cool and got a fine ass.' Period.

Just like Pac-Man though, my cold heart ran out, and her passive-aggressive comments and need for love or affection or something other than smart-assed lust caught up with me. Like Pac-Man, my invincibility ran out, the ghosts caught me when I got greedy, caught me like a limp dick. See, like in Common's dis track aimed at Ice Cube ('The Bitch in Yoo'), I found the bitch in me. The fearful, self-degrading, finger-pointing bitch in me that didn't want to get hurt.

Jeremy Relph

✳

```
*THE ART OF CONTESTED SPACES*
SCORE(1) HI-SCORE SCORE(2)
   0000   0000      1980

*HENRY JENKINS/KURT SQUIRE*
```

Below
Sid Meier's *Civilization* games depict
history as a succession of conflicts or
contests over land and other resources.
The interface allows players to survey
their conquered lands, assess their
resources, and suss out the defences
of neighbouring territories while keeping
their opponents' resources hidden.
This screen represents the Middle East;
its strategic location between Europe
and Asia makes it a highly volatile
region, much as it remains a contested
site in the real world. The top-down maps
encourage a global perspective, rather
than a focus on individualized experience.

Effective game design can yield spaces that encourage our exploration, provide resources for our struggles for dominance, evoke powerful emotions and encourage playfulness and sociability.

Let's try something bold. Let's start from the assumption that games are an important form of contemporary art. What kind of art are they? Most often, critics discuss games as a narrative art, as interactive cinema or participatory storytelling. But perhaps we should consider another starting point, viewing games as a spatial art with its roots in architecture, landscape painting, sculpture, gardening or amusement-park design.

Game worlds are totally constructed environments. Everything there was put on the screen for a purpose – shaping the game play or contributing to the mood and atmosphere or encouraging performance, playfulness, competition or collaboration. If games tell stories, they do so by organizing spatial features. If games stage combat, then players learn to scan their environments for competitive advantages. Game designers create immersive worlds with embedded rules and relationships among objects that enable dynamic experiences.

Games draw inspiration from sports (contests over goals or field position) and board games (contests won and lost according to movements around the game board); they also tap literary and cinematic genres that climax with spatial contests (the shootout in a western, the space battles in science fiction). A hybrid form, games get their focus on space both from sports and from stories.

Stripped to their simplest elements, the earliest digital games consisted of little more than contested spaces. Picture Pac-Man gobbling his way through a simple maze and trying to avoid getting caught by ghosts. As game technology improves, the potential for creating complex and compelling spaces seems unlimited. Strategy games, such as *Civilization* or *Age of Empires*, transform the entire globe into their game board, casting players as the rulers of expanding nation-states locked in a struggle for global domination. Modern equivalents for the backyard, fields and woodlands where previous generations played 'capture the flag', first-person shooters like *Castle Wolfenstein*, *Doom*, *Quake*, *Serious Sam* or *Unreal Tournament* pit players in primal struggles over more localized spaces, such as warehouses, rooms or corridors.

The shift from the top-down maps of *Civilization* to the through-the-gunsights perspective of the shooters suggests a much more immediate, moment-by-moment participation in the struggles for spatial dominance. Single-player games feature linear levels that are not meant to be explored, but rather 'cleared' of hostile creatures, while multi-player levels feature multiple overlapping paths with dangerous intersections. Exceptional players learn to 'read' tactical possibilities from the spaces themselves. Drawing on a concept from psychologist James Gibson, game designers design spaces or objects for their games which offer players certain 'affordances', spaces or objects embedded with potentials for actions, such as hiding and shooting at other players.

Bottom left

Half-Life creates a diverse array of contested spaces. Here, Freeman needs to enter a door on the other side of this pit. He can only do so by first throwing a grenade across this crevice in order to distract the three-headed monster. Hoping for a more immersive experience, *Half-Life* adopts a first-person perspective and offers a more adaptive environment; characters react to the sounds he makes and his tools can be repurposed to allow for more creative problem solving.

Bottom centre

Inspired by early graphics games, such as *Tetris*, *Snood* lets players fire brightly coloured icons at the screen, hoping to match up shapes, and clear the board. Successful players can move to more complex puzzle levels. *Snood* provides little narrative framing, encouraging players to find pleasure in process rather than story, yet the coloured shapes are given personalities, expressed through their shifting facial expressions, which add a dash of whimsy.

Bottom right

This image from *Morrowind* shows how spatial storytelling can play out on a micro level in the design of specific environments. Players choose among bridges and portals, and each decision has potential implications for situations the character encounters, the skills the character develops, the knowledge they acquire, and ultimately, the shape of their narrative experiences. This misty, cavernous landscape and the focus on natural materials (wood, hide or rock) reflect the genre's roots in J.R.R. Tolkien's *Lord of the Rings* books.

Although its plot resembles early maze games such as *Berzerk*, the action adventure game *Half-Life* uses backstory, interactivity, puzzles and atmosphere to make a rich game space. The protagonist, Gordon Freeman, finds himself trapped at the bottom of a nuclear research facility surrounded by mutated space aliens. His struggle to fight his way to the surface unfolds in an intricately designed, interactive, three-dimensional world of metallic surfaces, nuclear waste, expansive hallways and cramped ventilation ducts. *Half-Life* takes the player through a variety of atmospheres, resulting in a rise and fall of dramatic tension.

Some gamers feel nostalgic for the simplicity, immediacy and eloquence of early design solutions. Every element was carefully selected to minimize the demand for bytes and maximize player flexibility. Many independent game designers, such as *Blix*'s Eric Zimmerman or *Snood*'s David Dobson, have embraced a 'back to the basics' approach, stressing play mechanics and simple spaces over the 'bells and whistles' of corporate games. In modern art, minimalists reduced their options to the minimum number of colours, shapes, lines and textures; they were more interested in the physical surface of the canvas rather than in mimicking real-world perspectives. Dobson and Zimmerman are game minimalists, searching for the medium's simple core principles and stripping away unnecessary features.

Snood and *Blix* use simple rules to offer players unlimited play within limited game spaces, whereas *Civilization*, *Unreal Tournament* or *Morrowind* use more elaborate spaces to stage conflicts. Other games, inspired by *Dungeons and Dragons*, offer exploratory spaces, where players complete quests, solve challenges or collect treasures. In exploration games, player mastery over a level, by besting an enemy, completing a puzzle or simply pushing through the obstacle course, is rewarded by allowing access to the next spectacular world. Reflecting this fascination with spatial exploration, the designers scatter these worlds with 'Easter eggs' (hidden treasures and secret areas not initially obvious to casual players).

Below

In early electronic games, players were confined to one space, no more complex than a paper maze or a traditional gameboard. In *Berzerk* the player was trapped in a room surrounded by gun-toting aliens who attacked from every direction. Players learned which walls might serve as shields and which paths were dangerous dead-ends. *Berzerk's* world was hostile and claustrophobic, with little chance of long-term survival, since each path led to another room full of aliens. You played until you died, hanging on for dear life against the computer and seeing how high a score you could rack up.

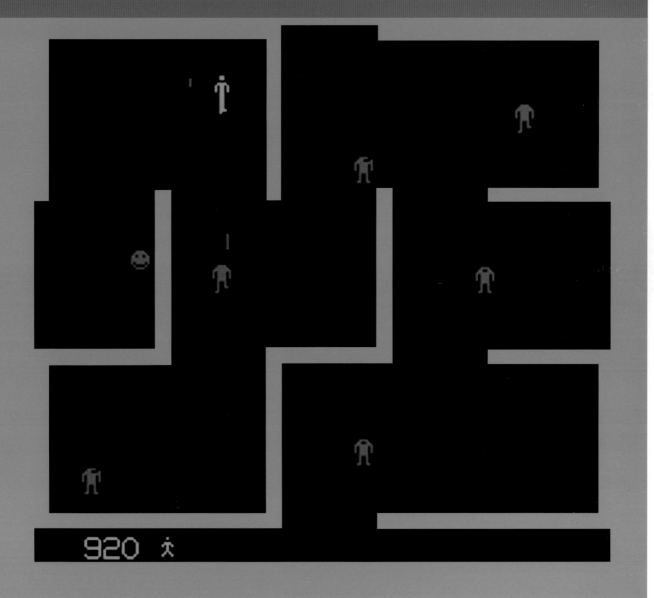

Centre

Shigeru Miyamoto's *Super Mario Brothers* sought to recreate a child's magical engagement with unknown spaces: 'When I was a child, I went hiking and found a lake. It was quite a surprise for me to stumble upon it. When I travelled around the country without a map, trying to find my way, stumbling on amazing things as I went, I realized how it felt to go on an adventure like this. The spirit, the state of mind of a kid when he enters a cave alone must be realized in the game. Going in, he must feel the cold of air around him. He must discover a branch off to one side and decide whether to explore it or not. Sometimes he loses his way.'

Bottom, left and centre

Set in a fully realized, visually distinctive representation of the land of the dead inspired by Mexican folk culture, art deco architecture, and film noir camerawork, *Grim Fandango* stars Manny Calavera, an employee of the Department of the Death, who is on a quest to uncover corruption in the department. Here, Manny visits a street fair, decked out in a double-breasted zoot suit, and talks to a clown. This scene evokes a carnivalesque atmosphere through its flamboyant colours, flowing lines of fabric, and folk art representations of callaveras (skulls).

Bottom right

Rayman 2 is a more recent exploration game which masks its hard rails through careful design. This path encourages visual exploration into the environment but limits the player's physical movements. As in the early Miyamoto games, the space remains a series of flat surfaces but the cartoonish abstraction of the protagonist helps to justify the stylization of the physical 'track' along which he moves. Several additional elements – butterflies that flit ahead of the protagonist or a waterfall he passes under – hint at greater depth without making a significant impact on game play.

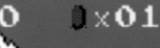

MARIO 000200 ⬛×01 WORLD 1-1 TIME 269

Building on early exploratory games, Shigeru Miyamoto, who masterminded the *Mario Brothers* and *Zelda* series for Nintendo, revitalized the medium with his focus on innovative virtual environments. The bright colours, friendly skies and beckoning caverns of *Super Mario Brothers* create a childlike realm that encourages play and exploration. Miyamoto rewards the player with magic mushrooms, gold coins, hidden treasures and secret worlds that can only be unlocked by inventive play. In *Game Over*, David Sheff explains how Miyamoto extensively charted his game space: 'When a game was nearly completed, he spread out its blueprints across a room full of tables that had been pushed together. The blueprint was the map of a game's pathways, corridors, rooms, secret worlds, trapdoors and myriad surprises. Miyamoto lived with it for days, travelling through the game in his mind.'

Miyamoto's focus on spatial exploration helped to define the aesthetic features that distinguished electronic games from previous forms of play. He innovated a genre known as the 'scroll game', where players move left to right through a space that unscrolls before them. Exploiting 3D modelling tools, more recent games seek stronger depth cues, allowing players to move through space in any direction including from foreground to background.

Game designers draw a distinction between games with 'hard rails', which tightly structure the player's movements to unfold a predetermined experience, and those with 'soft rails', which are multidirectional and multilinear. *Rayman 2*, a spatial exploration game with relatively hard rails, masks its prestructured trajectory through creative spatial design. The game makes effective use of off-screen space to hint at further adventures around the next corner. Its basic building blocks – caverns, tunnels, bridges, rivers, paths, ledges – provide narrative rationales for various constraints on our movement.

Game designers use spatial elements to set the initial terms for the player's experiences. Information essential to the story is embedded in objects such as books, carved runes or weapons. Artifacts such as jewels may embody friendship or rivalries or may become magical sources of the player's power. The game space is organized so that paths through the world guide or constrain action, making sure we encounter characters or situations critical to the narrative. Such characters may propose quests or reveal clues, but the player decides whether or not to accept those missions. Game designers refer to such devices as embedded information, finding that they allow for deeper and more flexible game experiences. As Tim Shafer, lead designer on LucasArts's *Grim Fandango*, explains, the challenge of game design is to 'lead the player along' a predetermined pathway without 'making them feel that they are being controlled'. Few, if any games, rival *Grim Fandango*'s artful meeting of this challenge.

THE ART OF CONTESTED SPACES

Bottom left

Deus Ex modelled many of its locations after real world spaces, such as Liberty Island in this early game level, complete with the New York skyline in the distance. A terrorist group has blown the head off the Statue of Liberty, and is holding a government agent hostage in the statue, a familiar scenario of contested space. As Warren Spector notes, this focus on real spaces set high expectations for players which the game designers struggled to meet.

Bottom centre

In *SSX*, the arrows, blowing flags, swooshing sounds, and sweeping camera movements convey snowboarding's speed and motion. Hidden spaces, such as the space beyond this arc or beneath a jump, build and release tension, shaping the rhythm of the action. Game engines frequently exaggerate players' movements and impact on the environment, as the swathe of plowed snow in this image reveals.

Bottom right, opposite page

In *Black & White*, Peter Molyneux wanted to introduce a stronger focus on choice and consequence. We start the game with a pristine world. The player controls a gigantic creature who affects the environment – rescuing children, ripping out trees, smashing houses or erecting buildings. In controlling this creature, the player competes with other gods for the devotion of the game's inhabitants. The villagers form moral judgments on the creature's actions based on a combination of deontology (the morality of the action in and of itself) and utility (the effect of the action on the community as a whole). Good moral choices transform the world into a flowering garden.

Many critics have assumed that gradual improvement in game graphics will ultimately make game spaces indistinguishable from their real-world counterparts. Yet, those game designers who explore photorealistic imagery often discover that achieving realism involves more than improving image resolution and may not be what players desire.

Deus Ex takes place in about a dozen environments, most of which are modelled after real spaces. Yet, as producer and director Warren Spector notes: 'Believable settings raised expectations to unrealistic levels.' Spector wanted every element, from the design of the space to the development of the interface, to contribute to a powerful sense of 'being there'. He argues that well-designed game environments present players with clear goals, so that the player is encouraged to identify problems and devise plans; each space has multiple entry and exit points; and there are always multiple paths around obstacles. According to Spector, these games create 'possibility spaces', spaces that provide compelling problems within an overarching narrative, afford creative opportunities for dealing with these problems and then respond to players' choices with meaningful consequences.

Games like *Tony Hawk 2* or *SSX* promise players a realistic sense of what it would be like to participate in extreme sports. Often, they start with the challenge of re-creating actual locales and arenas as well as duplicating styles and moves associated with specific sports stars. Sports game designers note that they are responding to player expectations shaped as much by watching the sports on television as by playing them directly, so they build into the games aspects of the broadcast experience, such as voice-over commentary or instant replays. Much as in actual snowboarding, game mastery demands mastery over the run, knowledge of the specific contours of the game space. Game designers provide bumps, jumps and ramps for players to perform tricks. The result is not realism but rather 'immersiveness'. The realistic elements contribute to our sense of being there, whereas various forms of exaggeration 'perfect' the real-world experience, making it even more exciting.

Many game designers are recruited from art schools and many continue to paint and to scan through art books searching for inspiration. As a consequence, a close consideration of game space reveals a broad range of aesthetic influences, including Expressionism (which maps emotions onto physical space) and Romanticism (which endows landscapes with moral qualities). As game designers dig deeper into these artistic traditions, they may develop more emotionally evocative and meaningful spaces.

The British game designer Peter Molyneux, who has been widely credited with helping to develop the 'god game' genre, has often told reporters that his inspiration came from a childhood spent watching anthills, disturbing the ground with his foot to force the ants to reroute or rebuild their environment and tormenting them with magnifying glasses. In his games, players exert divine control over the environment, indirectly controlling how the world's inhabitants behave. In Molyneux's *Black & White*, the player's choices have clearly defined consequences which are made manifest on the physical environment, much as the Romantic artists used landscapes to express allegorical or moral visions.

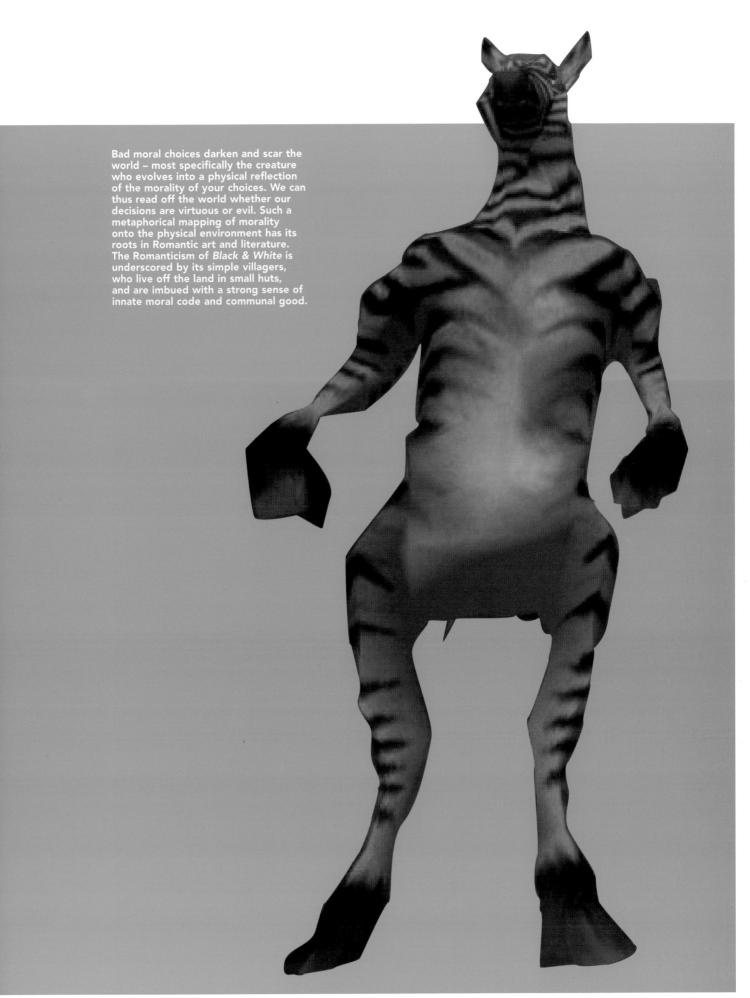

Bad moral choices darken and scar the world – most specifically the creature who evolves into a physical reflection of the morality of your choices. We can thus read off the world whether our decisions are virtuous or evil. Such a metaphorical mapping of morality onto the physical environment has its roots in Romantic art and literature. The Romanticism of *Black & White* is underscored by its simple villagers, who live off the land in small huts, and are imbued with a strong sense of innate moral code and communal good.

Top left

Brenda Laurel's *Secret Paths* games offered a very different representation of the natural environment. Laurel's company, Purple Moon, wanted to attract girls who they felt were being left behind in the digital revolution. If the boys' games encourage players to conceive of nature as an obstacle, Laurel's games depict nature as a healing force. Each Secret Path leads into another enchanted environment, where girls can search for insights into their emotional and social problems.

Bottom left

American McGee's *Alice* builds on our familiarity with other retellings of *Alice in Wonderland*. This nostalgia invites us to linger and explore Alice's richly detailed environments, yet the game's frenetic pace makes this impossible. The game's enclosed cavernous spaces, high toppling walls and disorienting mazes contribute to our sense of paranoia.

Top right

Giant's landscape seems otherworldly and the game depends upon a whimsical blend of science fictional and mythic elements (lasers, jet packs, bug-eyed aliens and monstrous giants). Much as Dali employed shading, depth cues and Renaissance perspective to construct his fantastical environments, the game space conforms to the laws of earthly physics which gives tangibility to its offbeat storyline.

Romantic influences might also be felt in the elemental images of earth, water, fire and air running through *Sacrifice*. The game centres around the competition between gods and demons for human souls. Such games celebrate heroic struggles to master inhospitable environments, depicting nature as a destructive force that actively thwarts human will.

Brenda Laurel's *Secret Paths* games, designed for girls, offer a more nurturing relationship to the natural world, promising possibilities for contemplation rather than mastery. Laurel explained that girls wanted a place to go where they could daydream: 'they thought that the garden/forest would be a place where they could find out things that would be important to them.'

Surrealism is another modern art movement that has influenced game design. The Surrealists created dreamlike images which nevertheless followed many conventions of representational art, often deploying familiar stories (such as those in the Bible) as a basis for psychologically complex, symbol-laden environments. Similarly, game designers exploit the graphic possibilities of 3D modelling to create immersive environments that are vivid and tangible and yet totally imaginary.

American McGee rose to prominence as a level designer, making memorable contributions to *Quake* and *Doom*. When Electronic Arts offered him the chance to develop his own game, he turned towards an unanticipated topic – Lewis Carroll's *Alice in Wonderland*. In the distinctly gothic *Alice*, his protagonist dwells in a mental asylum, having been driven insane by her inability to discern whether her Wonderland adventures are real or hallucinations. She is drawn back to do battle with the Red Queen and her evil minions. We know these spaces – the rabbit's hole, the lake of tears, the Red Queen's garden, and so forth – from our childhood, yet they are disfigured and distorted by Alice's demented perspective.

Giants: Citizen Kabuto is another game set in a Surrealist landscape with fantastic creatures; its icons seem to drip off the screen like Salvador Dali's melting clocks. It unfolds in a world largely devoid of manmade structures, a landscape of earth, rocks and sparse vegetation, rendered in bright blues, yellows and greens.

As Steven Poole argues in *Trigger Happy*, few games have really embraced the Surrealist aesthetic. While many games borrow visual cues from Expressionism, most are relatively conservative when it comes to modelling reality, bending to, rather than eschewing, basic physical laws. *Giants: Citizen Kabuto* suggests how Surrealist elements might enrich future games.

Bottom right

Sacrifice, known for its elemental images, establishes a stark contrast between the cool blue-green water and the fiery red sky. Compared to many action games, where the human protagonist dominates the image and remains central at all times, players in *Sacrifice* bounce among angles. The human figure is off-centered and dwarfed by his environment, suggesting the limited power of mankind in this cosmic struggle.

Top

The Sims focuses on familiar spaces which look and feel like the homes where the players themselves live. We are thus encouraged to use the simulator for social experimentation, modelling our own interpersonal relationships with friends, lovers or family members, and testing alternative social strategies for coping with everyday conflicts and tensions. The system is robust enough to enable players to construct many different kinds of domestic arrangements, including the same-sex relationship depicted here.

At the same time, players never fully control their characters. They suggest possibilities for action or shape their environment to encourage certain choices, but their instructions are read against preprogrammed values, needs, urges, goals and priorities which are the basic defining traits of these characters.

Centre

In this cityscape from *Shenmue*, the buildings and walls are made of hard, cold surfaces like brick and cement, and painted in muted colours. As Ryo walks along these lonely streets, we hear the distant sounds of dogs barking and cats meowing, as well as the more immediate noise of his footsteps on the slushy pavement. Ryo can duck into the telephone booth in the distance to contact his allies. The kitten wandering the street becomes a mechanism for initiating his love interest, and he will meet an elderly man who trains him in karate in the park around the corner. Despite rather linear game play, what one carries away from *Shenmue* is its overwhelming melancholy and lyrical images.

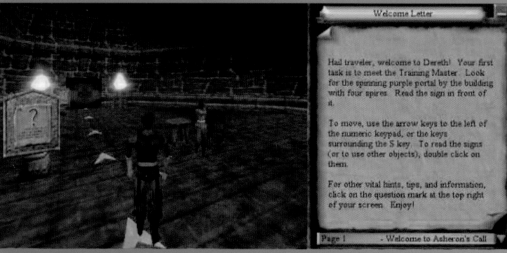

Opposite page bottom

This *Asheron's Call* interface was designed to encourage a high degree of social interaction, with a strong focus on communication between players, as expressed through the chat window, the radar which can help locate other players, and the dove icon which communicates the player's aggressive or peaceful moods. This pub is empty – a common occurrence in online worlds. Designers have found that players tend to gather in areas that fulfil particular functions, like shops that sell equipment, fountains that heal life or crossroads where they can meet other players, rather than in environments that are 'designed' for socializing.

This game world is approximately the size of Rhode Island and would take nearly a day to run across. *Asheron's Call* contains a wide variety of spaces, ranging from civilized areas, populated cities, strategic outposts, frontier areas, and wilderness areas – each of which gains their meaning in part through players' responses to the environment.

Game designers increasingly focus on the overall 'mood' or emotional colour of their projects. Hoping to produce games that can provide a broader range of emotional experiences, they draw inspiration from classic melodrama, where elements of the *mise en scène* become emotional correlatives for the protagonist's woes.

Yu Suzuki situates characters in more 'everyday' environments. His epic role-playing game *Shenmue* is set in a small Japanese village, circa 1986. The game's adolescent protagonist, Ryo, struggles against the men who murdered his father. Grey skies and snowy streets contribute to the game's sad, contemplative mood, expressing Ryo's experience of mourning and loss.

Myst, the dream project of Rand and Robyn Miller, was another game that received high praise for its atmospheric design. The artfulness of *Myst* invites us to linger and contemplate, like visitors in a museum. *Myst's* reputation as a 'thinking person's game' ultimately has less to do with its puzzles than with its amber colour scheme, its Rembrandt-like play with light and shadows, and its fascination with the textures of the material world.

Many people who don't know much about games assume they are socially isolating, that players always play against the computer. Solo play is one mode among many. Videogames originated in arcades before being marketed in the home; many preserve opportunities for spectacular performances best appreciated among friends. Playing alone often becomes a way of honing skills that are then deployed in shared competition. New interfaces encourage players to dance, beat drums, shake maracas or manipulate turntables; these games are called 'embarrassment sims' because they create amusing situations for parties. Multi-player games, such as *Asheron's Call*, borrow lessons from urban planners to create opportunities for sociability, becoming the centre of vast 'virtual communities', and other games, such as *The Sims*, encourage players to create content actively and share it with the fan community, designing clothes, objects and buildings that constitute these virtual worlds. The *Star Wars* multi-player online game sought player advice from the very beginning of the design process. Many next-generation games like *Neverwinter Nights* and *Morrowind* are packaged with powerful but easy-to-use editing tools that are expected to be more successful than the game content itself.

As players engage more directly in the design process, the line between gamers and designers begins to dissolve. To participate fully, players will need to learn more about the art of game design. Effective game design can yield spaces that encourage our exploration, provide resources for our struggles for dominance, evoke powerful emotions and encourage playfulness and sociability. This art owes much to previous traditions, including those of painting, architecture and urban design, but it also takes advantage of the unique properties of emerging digital media. Games have always been an art of contested spaces; video and digital games have now pushed that art to a new level of aesthetic accomplishment.

Henry Jenkins
Kurt Squire

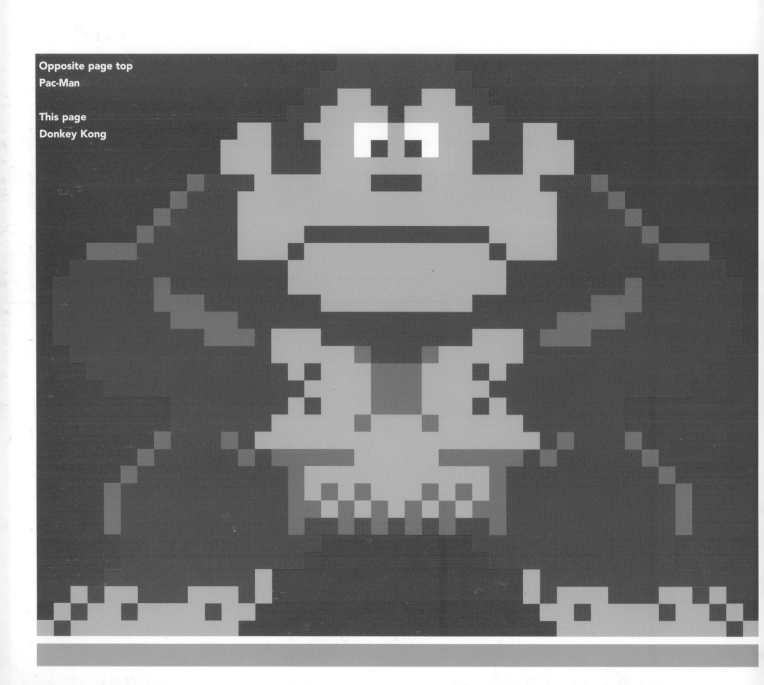

Opposite page top
Pac-Man

This page
Donkey Kong

Videogame character design is potentially a very deep and difficult art: it is the art of designing people, or at least beings, into whose shoes we can enjoy stepping.

A videogame character is the game's star: the central figure that you control and, to some extent perhaps, become. Is a videogame character, then, like a movie star? Not really. Film actors are chosen from a pre-existing pool of humans: you can give them a haircut and a makeover, and dress them how you like, but at bottom the person's a given. The star of a videogame, on the other hand, is invented: built completely from the ground up. Is a videogame character like a character in a novel? Again, not really. Whereas a novelist will normally only provide a few salient features of a person's appearance and let the reader's imagination do the rest, a videogame character must be determinedly individuated and given a complete, solid visual form.

The first videogame 'character' of all was Pac-Man (1980). Before then, in games such as *Space Invaders*, the player had merely controlled spaceships, gun turrets or other mechanical devices. Suddenly, though, the player of *Pac-Man* controlled a being: an animated, eating thing. The game's designer, Toru Iwatani, says that he got the idea for Pac-Man's form after eating a slice of pizza and seeing the shape that was left. 'I designed Pac-Man to be the simplest character possible, without any features such as eyes or limbs. Rather than defining the image of Pac-Man for the player, I wanted to leave that to each player's imagination.'

As technology improved, however, game designers wanted to individuate their characters more fully. The year after *Pac-Man* saw the first videogame with a fully humanoid character – Shigeru Miyamoto's *Donkey Kong* (1981), with its era-defining mustachioed hero, later to be christened Mario. Mario's style was still dictated by technological considerations, however. Because of the low resolution offered by videogame systems back then, character designers only had a limited number of pixels – the little squares of light that make up the visual image – to play with. Miyamoto gave Jumpman (as he was called then) a hat, simply because the technology didn't allow for animated hair; the character wore dungarees to differentiate his red arms from his blue legs. Once this style had been established, it remained the same for two decades, even as Mario's form became plumped out and solidified with modern 3D graphics.

In Japan, videogames have strong aesthetic and commercial links with manga (comic books) and anime (animated cartoon films). And their peculiar style of character-drawing has had a very strong influence on Japanese, and subsequently on one strain of Western, videogames. Anime in particular uses a so-called 'deformed' style for its humanoid characters: they have huge heads and eyes, and tiny bodies. In the early days of videogames, technological considerations forced designers into exactly the same style. With so few pixels to play with, Shigeru made Mario 'deformed', with a big head and squat legs. Even so, Mario became such a successful icon that, by 1990, a survey determined that the virtual Italian plumber was recognized by more American children than Mickey Mouse.

Many if not most of the best-loved videogames are those that feature good characters – Crash Bandicoot (*Crash Bandicoot 3: Warped*, 1998), Mario, Parappa the singing dog (*Parappa the Rapper 2*, 2001) – or personable imaginary beasts – in the *Pokémon* series, for instance. Nintendo in particular is recognized as having a good stock of reusable characters – in fact the US and Japanese launch of the GameCube in 2001 was the only occasion on which a Nintendo machine was launched without a game featuring Mario. Instead, Nintendo developed a hitherto minor character taken from its fictional canon: Mario's brother Luigi, star of the ghostbusting game *Luigi's Mansion* (2001).

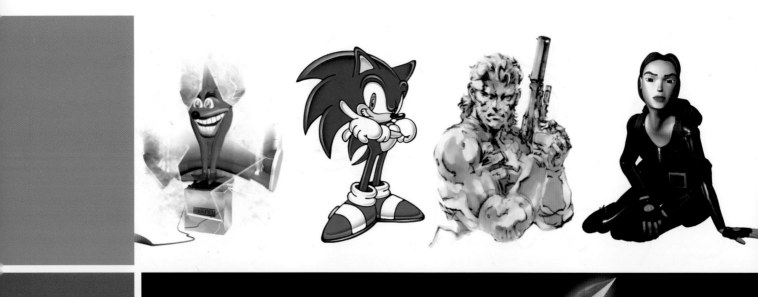

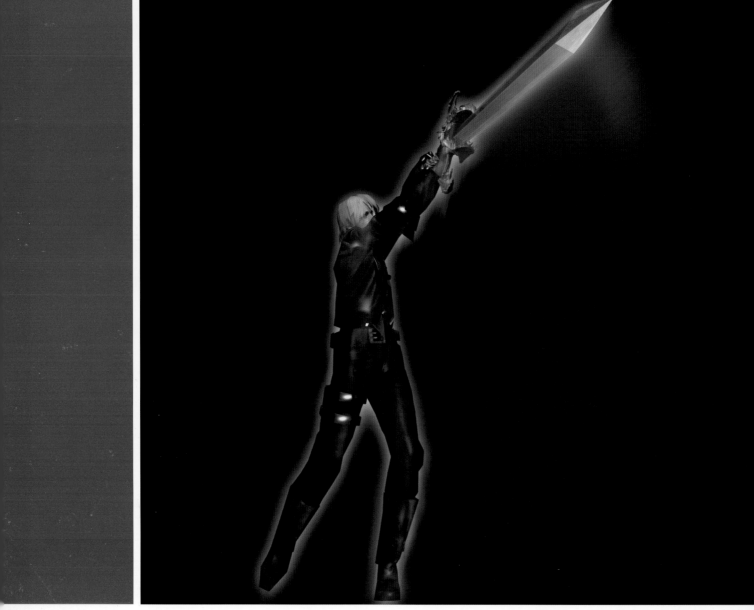

But what do all these 'good characters' have in common? At first sight, there seems to be a world of difference between Pac-Man and a modern videogame character such as Lara Croft in *Tomb Raider Chronicles* (2000). That is certainly true if you regard these characters as traditional static pictures. But videogames are a kinetic artform. And, in this sense, Pac-Man and Lara do share one important attraction. If you swing the joystick to move Pac-Man around his maze, he opens and shuts his mouth automatically. If you press a button to make Lara walk forward, she does so with a fluid, hip-swinging motion that is the result of hundreds of frames of painstaking digital animation. Witness, too, the way that Solid Snake in *Metal Gear Solid 2* (2001) crouches, rolls and leaps around with stealthy purpose, or the highly stylized, gothic-cool, cloak-swirling swordplay and gun-wielding of the archly named Dante in *Devil May Cry* (2001). This is dynamic attraction: a few simple controls result in absorbing, complex movements.

Dynamic attraction must always be balanced by purely pictorial or iconic attraction. Characters such as Crash Bandicoot or Sonic the Hedgehog (in *Sonic Adventure 2*, 2001) obviously borrow heavily from cartoon styles. Sonic was allegedly a deliberate crossing of Felix the Cat with Mickey Mouse, while Crash obeys the cartoon tradition of animals that look nothing like their real-life counterparts. Both Crash and Sonic have big heads, saucer eyes, cheeky grins and small bodies.

On the other hand, characters such as Lara Croft or Solid Snake borrow from cinematic conventions of costume and coolness. It is surely no coincidence that *Metal Gear Solid 2*'s cigarette-loving, husky-voiced hero shares part of his name with Kurt Russell's character in the film *Escape from New York*, Snake Pliskin: Solid Snake has the stubble-jawed determination and efficiently muscled physique of all good action-movie stars.

A good videogame character is one that the player likes, one whose iconic appearance and movements combine to give us pleasure. And since the character is under our control, if we like him (or her), we must also feel somehow protective, and anxious lest we cause the character harm through our own inadequacy. And so a good character, as well as being aesthetically pleasing, constitutes one very strong motivation for playing the videogame well: we want Solid Snake to avoid the booby traps and defeat the terrorists.

The mainstream of videogame character design, however, has tended to follow a rut, especially in the tradition of more 'realistic'-looking characters that has grown up in parallel to the Japanese 'deformed' aesthetic and the global influence of cartoon animation. There is an identifiable strand of what we might generally call sci-fi S&M. Much is made of Lara Croft's generous chest, but her design is positively monastic compared to that of Ivy from the fighting game *Soul Calibur* (1999), a whip-wielding dominatrix in a tight basque.

Joanna Dark, the heroine of the espionage-themed shooter *Perfect Dark* (2000), is also part of this bog-standard fetishism. Artwork of the seductively reclining spy shows an outfit that is designed with hilarious disregard for practicality. Her black leather-and-plastic boots have absurdly high heels; her thighs and forearms are encased in articulated metal tubing. This woman could not possibly succeed in missions of stealthy infiltration: the metallic clanking of her outfit would give her away immediately, and then she'd fall over in her silly footwear.

Nor is the situation much better for a great number of male videogame characters, who are largely dumb, muscled grunts – a tradition refreshingly parodied by the sardonic Duke Nukem in numerous games including *Duke Nukem Forever* (2001) – when they're not actually cyborgs (giving your character permanently glued-on cybergoggles or half a metal face obviously solves an aesthetic problem on one level). The central characters of slightly more cerebral adventure games, such as Ryo in *Shenmue* (2000) or Eike in *Shadow of Memories* (2000), are merely blank-faced teenagers stuck in a fashion timewarp. Solid Snake is the best of this bunch, and only his curiously retro mullet haircut saves him from clichéd iconicism. Videogames have excelled at dynamic character design – in the rolls, jumps and runs that make us believe we are controlling a living creature – but they have barely scratched the surface in terms of creating people that are believable and interesting to look at.

**Opposite page
and this page**

Lara Croft
Tomb Raider

Perhaps there will be no need even to try in the future, as there is an increasing trend to digitize the faces of real people and map them onto virtual avatars, beginning with *Goldeneye* (1997), a seminal James Bond-themed shooter in which actors from the movie, including Robbie Coltrane and Sean Bean, were recognizable secondary characters in the game itself. Another option is to create a sort of digital photofit made up from parts of various desirable Hollywood actors, as seems to have been the case in the debut digital feature film made by Japanese videogame company Squaresoft, *Final Fantasy: The Spirits Within* (2001). If the level of visual technology used in that film is within reach of videogames five years hence, it can only be hoped that the creativity of character designers will have improved accordingly.

Videogame character design is, of course, potentially a very deep and difficult art: it is the art of designing people, or at least beings, into whose shoes we can enjoy stepping. But the increasing technological power available to the videogame designer also presents a challenge, because photographic realism is not necessarily desirable. After all, if a videogame character represents a fully detailed individual, there is a danger that there will be no purchase for our psychological projection. Perhaps we cannot become a character who looks too self-contained.

Despite Angelina Jolie's courageous attempt at impersonating her, for example, Lara Croft will always remain, to some extent, a deliberate abstraction, an animated conglomeration of sexual and attitudinal signs – breasts, hotpants, shades, thigh holsters. She needs to offer a comparatively blank canvas, because that is what encourages the player's psychological projection. So too with Solid Snake, who looks sufficiently like a lethal-but-sensitive counter-terrorist agent to make us engage in his fictional context, but not too much like someone we might take exception to for purely human, arbitrary reasons. The challenge for videogame character designers in the future, then, is to engage us while continuing to leave room for our imagination.

Steven Poole

This page
Quake III

Opposite page
Star Wars Galaxies

In a virtual environment as complex as a massively multi-player online world, whose success depends entirely on player interaction, developers recognize the player base as a strategic asset.

The development cycle for a videogame, circa 2002, is 18 months, from the generation of the design specification to the release of the product (production typically involves 12–20 people, with costs ranging from $5–$7 million). But for many games, and particularly the stronger-selling PC titles, that process begins before the 'official' development period, and extends afterwards, with a continuous stream of two-way feedback between the developers and players.

Perhaps the most extreme example of front-loaded game design is the forthcoming multi-player online world based on *Star Wars*, which is being built by Verant, the leading developer in this genre, and LucasArts. When it is launched in 2003, *Star Wars Galaxies* is expected to attract more than a million subscribers – based on *Everquest*'s usage statistics, that means more than 300,000 simultaneous players at peak usage. The environment is massive – it will take weeks or months to traverse without 'hyperspace' shortcuts – and will support a fully-fledged economic and political system. Players will develop their characters by scaling a number of intersecting skill trees (engine mechanics, armour production, combat, knowledge in the Ways of the Force, etc).

But even as the basic technology is being built, players are already a vital part of the design process. Immediately after the development deal was signed, Verant set up a message board *starwarsgalaxies. station.sony.com/starwars_dev_boar ds.html*, both to communicate news about the game in progress and to solicit feedback from a 'hardcore' player population with over ten million man-hours of collective experience with games in this genre.

In a virtual environment as complex as a massively multi-player online world, whose success depends entirely on player interaction, developers recognize the player base as a strategic asset. The dynamics of these games are rapidly evolving, and many of the parameters have yet to be defined. When in doubt, designers turn to the message boards to tap players' perspectives on the pros and cons of specific features, and aspects that could be improved. These are, after all, the people who are going to be inhabiting this virtual environment on a week-to-week basis when the product is launched, and who will determine its success. The game belongs to the players, as much as to the developer. So it is in the developers' interest to keep players in the loop, as the game takes shape, and to leverage their experience. This is not a marketing ploy ('Make them feel valued and they'll evangelize the product to their friends'), although it does generate good will. It is part of the core design process.

Within existing technologies in well-established genres, the player base is even more actively involved in the design and evolution of videogames. First-person shooters such as *Quake III Arena* and *Unreal Tournament* are built on engines that have evolved over years and have been passed between programming teams and a population of gamers who customize and often improve the game, just as its sequel is being planned. Player innovations are thus incorporated into the next version of the product.

Perhaps the most salient example of this phenomenon is in-game artificial intelligence, one of the great engineering hurdles in any game. In first-person shooters, there is a marked difference between real and computer-generated opponents – human opponents are invariably smarter, less predictable and more challenging to play against. There is no comparison between a multi-player death-match (elimination combat with up to eight people on the same 3D map) and a single-player game with AI opponents. Because of this discrepancy, first-person shooters are, *defacto*, online multi-player games; several have dispensed with single-player mode altogether.

AI, however, like all engineering challenges, is subject to the 'million monkeys' syndrome: put a million gamers into a room with an open, extensible game engine, and sooner or later, one of them will come up with the first-person shooter equivalent of *Hamlet*. In the case of Id Software's *Quake II*, it was a plug-in called the ReaperBot, a fiendishly clever and intelligent AI opponent written by a die-hard gamer named Steven Polge (who was subsequently employed by Id's main rival, Epic Games, to write AI for the *Unreal* engine). Polge's Reaperbot was far and away the best *Quake* opponent anyone (inside or outside Id Software) had ever seen, and the plug-in rapidly disseminated within the million-strong player population, who quickly began hacking away at its bugs, even though such modifications were technically illegal. Needless to say, these improvements in game AI were incorporated into the core technology of first-person shooters, to everyone's benefit, not least the game companies'.

Most of the players who tinker with combat games aren't programmers. They don't have to be, because the editing and customization tools in today's games require no programming skill whatsoever. Levels of combat games can be constructed in a couple of hours by anyone familiar with basic game play. Real-time strategy games offer similar capabilities. New maps, with custom constellations of opposing forces, can be generated with a graphical user interface.

Notably, historical and quasi-historical simulations like Sid Meier's *Gettysburg* allow gamers to replay military conflicts under different conditions ('What if General Lee had been there?' 'What if Pickett hadn't charged?'). That is not to say that the software delivers any definitive answer that a military tactician could not. The point is, the flexibility of the framework allows and encourages non-expert, individual players to ask the questions, explore the solution space around a particular scenario, and create new scenarios that might not have occurred to the game's designers.

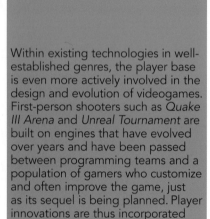

In a commercial context, this tool-based, user-driven activity extends the life of the game: the longer people play the game, the longer they talk about it, effectively marketing it to their friends. Will Wright, author of the best-selling *Sim City* series, compares the spread of a product in this fashion to a virus: 'Double the contagious period,' he says, 'and the size of the epidemic goes up by an order of magnitude. If I can get people to play for twice as long, I sell ten times as many copies.' Wright's formula bears out on the bottom line – his latest game, *The Sims*, has spawned two expansion packs and racked up $340 million in sales since its 1998 release.

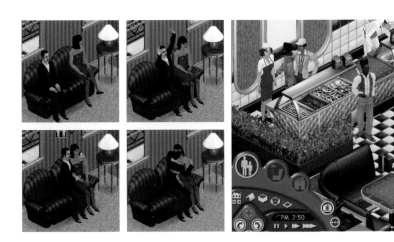

**Opposite page
and this page**

The Sims

The Sims, which scales Wright's *Sim City* down to the neighbourhood level, is noteworthy because it illustrates the level of engagement a game can achieve when its designers incorporate player feedback and collaboration before, during and after the release of the product. Four months before the game shipped, its developers released tools that allowed players to create custom objects for the game's virtual environment: architecture, props and custom characters. These tools were rapidly disseminated among *Sim City* players, who began creating custom content immediately. In the months leading up to the game's release, a network of player-run websites sprang up to showcase and exchange 'handcrafted' Sims objects and custom characters. By the time the game was released, there were 50 Sims fan sites, 40 artists pumping content into the pipeline, and 50,000 people collecting that content. A quarter of a million boxes flew off the shelves in the first week. A year later, there are dozens of people programming tools for Sims content creators, 150 independent content producers, half a million collectors, and millions of players reading 200 fan sites in 14 languages.

At this point, more than 90 per cent of *The Sims*' content is produced by the player population which systematically trains itself, generating more sophisticated content as it learns. This is a completely bottom-up, distributed, self-organizing process – none of these people are on the Maxis payroll. So, if these people aren't being paid by game developers (the reverse, in fact), why do they invest hundreds or thousands of hours in mastering the minutiae of these games? The dynamics that drive mastery and knowledge exchange in and around computer games derive from the social ecology of videogames. Tools and editing modes allow players to create assets (levels, modifications, 'skins' or character models) to extend the game experience. But more important than the stand-alone benefit of these assets is their value as social currency. The creator of a popular level, object or plug-in may not receive monetary remuneration. But he garners notice, and even acclaim, from fellow gamers.

Game modifications, or 'mods' are reviewed on thousands of game sites, from fan pages to high-traffic news destinations like GameSpy. These rotating showcases serve dual functions. For gamers wanting to download new content, they serve to sift for quality. For content creators, they offer widespread exposure. Because game culture is global, well-designed mods are lauded by an international array of websites in half a dozen languages. Even game levels and skins, which require less time and skill, are circulated on six continents (probably seven – field researchers in Antarctica have satellite web access, and a lot of time on their hands).

But even on a more local, limited basis, player-generated content circulates among peer groups. New levels, skins and modifications provide social fodder, and bring novelty to the networked game marathons that are now ubiquitous in college dorms, high-school computer labs, and offices populated by tech-savvy twenty-somethings. This explains why, at the height of the dot.com boom, there were lots of news stories about companies where 24-year-olds laboured late into the night. It was true that you could find programmers writing code at 11pm on a Thursday. But at that hour there was a lot of *Quake* on the company LAN.

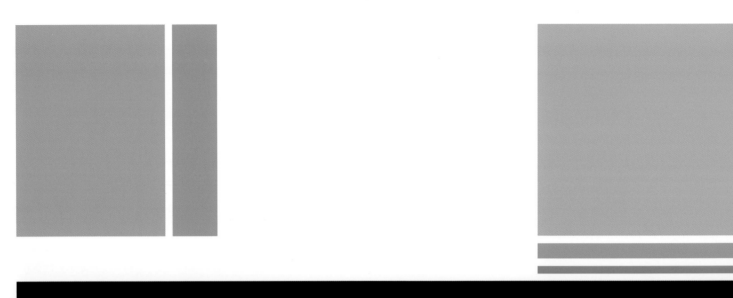

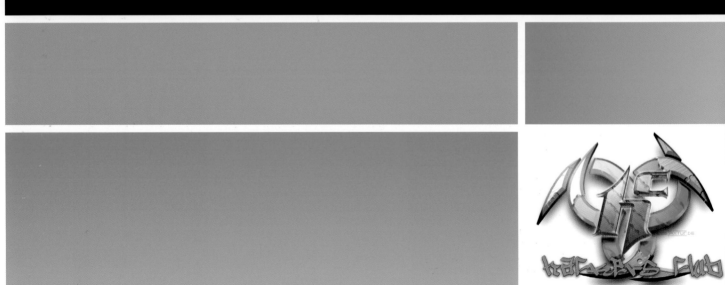

Competition (formal and informal) is the keystone of videogame culture, and motivates casual and hardcore gamers alike to hone their skills and evolve new strategies. Online game tournaments have grown into quasi-professional events, with top gamers earning substantial cash prizes. There is, in fact, a profit-making organization, the CyberAthlete Professional League, *www.thecpl.com*, to handle worldwide marketing and promotion for these events, which are sponsored by technology companies (Intel, Microsoft, Elsa, Logitech and Altec Lansing) and cater to the league's demographic (97 per cent of the CPL's players are male, mostly under 30 and unmarried). Blow-by-blow tournament coverage is available on dedicated news sites like Esports *www.esports-america.com*, the *Sports Illustrated* of PC gaming.

In videogame culture, status is easily established, readily compared and quantifiable. Every game ends with a winner and some losers. Tournament players are ranked. Player-created content is not only reviewed, but downloaded and therefore measurably popular. The author of a game level may have an internally driven sense of accomplishment, but he also knows that 18,431 people are playing his song. He gets laudatory e-mails from strangers. His friends ask him for level-building advice. A level designer he's never met, but whose work he admires, asks if he'd be interested in teaming up on a *CounterStrike* modification.

It is this web of relationships between players that sustains the videogame industry, no less than the latest 3D engine, facial-animation algorithm, or high-speed graphics card. These group dynamics are best represented by the vast network of self-organized combat clans that vie for dominance on the Internet. No game company told players to form clans – they just emerged, in the beta test for *Quake*, and have persisted for years. There are thousands of them. The smallest have five members; the largest have hundreds, and have developed their own politics, hierarchies and systems of government. They are essentially tribal – each has a name (usually tending towards the flamboyant: Enterprise Wrecking Crew, Dangerous Armed Warfare Guild, Pimps with Grenades), its own history, monikers, signs of identification (logos and team graphics). Clans do occasionally cluster into transnational organizations, adopting a shared moniker across national boundaries and a loose federalist structure. Generally, however, clans are comprised of players in the same country, because proximity reduces network lag. In games that require quick responses, this is an important factor.

Although most clans revolve around first-person combat games, there are hundreds of clans plotting against one another in real-time strategy games like *Age of Empires*, *HomeWorld* and *Space Empires* – *StarCraft* alone has 165 competing clans. Because strategy games are more nuanced than squad-based combat, clans in this genre tend to maintain more elaborate websites that go into some detail about the clan's history, rules, chain of command, custom maps and treaties with other clans (some clans even create password-protected areas where their allies can access strategic and diplomatic communication).

The clan network is a highly co-operative system because clans have a clear set of shared goals. Regardless of who wins or loses, they are mutually dependent on the shared spaces where gaming occurs, whether those spaces are maintained by gamers for gamers, such as ClanBase *www.clanbase.com/faq.php#what*, or owned and operated by game publishers, like Sony, Electronic Arts or Blizzard Entertainment, the developer of hit games such as *StarCraft*, *WarCraft* and *Diablo II*.

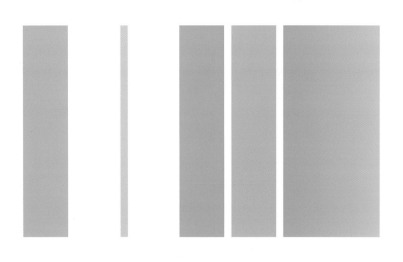

Opposite page and this page

Diablo II

Blizzard is a salient example for networked simulation mavens, because the company dedicates as much attention to nurturing competition between groups and individuals as it does to developing hit titles. When customers buy a copy of *Diablo II*, they don't just get a string of ones and zeroes on a CD. They get access to Battle.net *www.battle.net/intro.shtml*, a huge multi-player gaming platform Blizzard maintains for its customers at no additional hourly or monthly charge. Players simply select the Battle.net option from within the game, and are instantly connected to a worldwide network where they can chat, challenge opponents, initiate multi-player games, and download new maps, exchange ideas, strategies and tactics with other gamers, and participate in online tournaments. Gamers actually spend more time with pre- and post-game banter in the chat lobby than playing the game itself, and Battle.net's messaging system is designed to foster many levels and varieties of group communication. In addition to loitering in the public chat lobby, players can cluster in private communication channels. Each player can also designate up to 25 Battle.net members as 'friends', and keep track of whether they're logged onto the system.

Compared to the code that drives the game itself, Battle.net isn't hugely sophisticated. But it is the cultural infrastructure that invests players in the game, and keeps them playing. Maybe none of your friends owns a copy of *Diablo II* – it doesn't matter, there is a vibrant game-playing community ready to absorb you. And not only will it absorb you, but it will display your character's experience level like a badge, match you up against players with similar degrees of skill, and calculate your rank should you decide to participate in either low-level or high-level tournament ladders.

This cultural infrastructure is built into the experience, by design, and is recognized as a huge factor in Blizzard's success. The Battle.net ecosystem is actively nurtured, not as an afterthought or public service, but as an integral aspect of corporate strategy. The 'soft stuff' is not dismissed as non-profitable. It is budgeted, staffed, maintained, patched and extended, no less than the underlying game engine. Blizzard's products are videogames. But the social dynamics of a networked player population are the backbone of its business.

This is even more true of companies like Electronic Arts, Sony and Microsoft, which maintain persistent multi-player worlds for nearly half a million gamers on a subscription basis. Unlike most games, whose playing fields exist only while participants are actively engaged, multi-player online worlds like *Everquest*, *Ultima Online* or *Asheron's Call* persist, whether or not an individual player is logged on at any given time. The virtual environment is not something that vanishes when you stop playing – there are forces (some internal, some resulting from other player's actions) continuously at work. This sense of persistence gives the game depth, and is psychologically magnetic: the player is compelled to return habitually (even compulsively) to the environment, lest some new opportunity or crisis arise.

Compared to transient multi-player environments (i.e. combat and strategy games), the experience is qualitatively different. The world is dynamic, and therefore less predictable. More importantly, the duration of a single game is extended over the course of days, weeks or months. Players arrive in an environment knowing that action may flare and subside, but that the game is not going to be over in a few hours, and as a result, gain a sense of what it is like to be embroiled in a particular set of circumstances on a day-to-day basis – a human experience almost impossible to simulate in accelerated time.

Furthermore, the persistence of the environment allows players to develop their characters' identities within these worlds, which all conform to the conventions of role-playing games (RPGs). In an RPG, a player's progress is represented not by geographical movement (as in console adventure games like *Mario* or *Tomb Raider*, where the object is to get from point A to point B, defeating enemies along the way), but by the development of his or her character, who earns experience points by overcoming in-game challenges. At certain milestone point-tallies, the character is promoted to a new experience level, gaining strength, skill and access to new weapons and tactics – but also attracting more powerful enemies. The better the player becomes, the more challenging his opponents become. Thus, the player scales a well-constructed learning curve over several months as he builds his level one character into a highly skilled, fully equipped level-50 powerhouse. Unsurprisingly, players are highly invested in the characters they have built up. On a purely pragmatic level, those virtual personas represent hundreds of hours of invested time (which is why high-level *Everquest* characters sell for thousands of dollars on Ebay).

This page
Quake III

While he or she acquires experience and skill, the player is also networking on a number of levels. In these games, it is almost impossible to go it alone – the hazards of the environment necessitate the formation of small foray groups, or parties of four to six players. In addition, larger groups of players agglomerate into guilds ranging from a few dozen to upwards of a hundred affiliated characters. Like clans in the combat and strategy genres, these groups are tribal. They evolve their own customs and leadership structures. They form alliances and declare wars with other guilds. Some are peaceful and welcome new members. Others are roving bands of thugs who relish the opportunity to annihilate beginners should they mistakenly wander into parts of the game world where player-killing is allowed.

But then, on a basic level, this is what makes the massively multi-player online world go round – the standard societal tensions that inform any city-sized population (*Everquest* has a bigger population than Miami, Pittsburgh or Cincinnati). There is crime – and a collective response to crime. There is politics, and the complex web of rivalries, obligations and conflicts that implies. In a persistent online world, players build not only skills but reputations. Veteran characters have status by virtue of sheer strength and experience. But beyond that, long-time players have built reputations and connections – bonds of co-operation and friendship keep them rooted in the environment long after they have mastered the intricacies of game play.

J. C. Herz

This essay was adapted from a paper prepared for the National Defense University in August 2001, in response to a Defense Science Board review of the United States military's technological infrastructure and preparedness for 21st-century warfare. In response to the committee's queries about the technical sophistication of the videogame industry, the author argued that it was not hardware or software that drives innovation in videogames. Rather, it is the intersection of open architecture and on-line social dynamics that drives the medium forward. A highly networked, self-organizing player population is given the tools to customize and extend games, create new levels, modifications and characters. What emerges is a decentralized culture that rapidly learns, adapts and selects for best practices. This culture and its processes are perhaps the industry's greatest assets, and provide a counterpoint to the technological processes of a large, bureaucratic defence culture.

In the wake of September 11 2001, the contrast between centralized and decentralized modes of action, and the gap between the military's needs and capabilities, has never been more keenly felt – and reality has never seemed less virtual.

Episode 1015
Ken Thain
Unreal Tournament
Engine

Int. apartment – Brooklyn, NY
Voice of the narrator, Katie Salen, is
heard over the sounds of Quake.

The phone rang. It was London calling
with an invitation to write a piece for
a collection of essays on the history
and culture of videogames. Could
I write something about movies and
games? The deadline was tight, ten
days and counting…

Quickly, I scanned my mental inventory
of possible topics. What about a
piece on the history of the links in
subject matter between videogames
and film? I could offer a close detailing
of the first games to use movies as
their inspiration. This would include
a look at *Tron*, which successfully
connected the experiences of game
players and filmgoers, much in the
way that the movie and game of
GoldenEye or *Jurassic Park* and *Turok*
did. I would, of course, have some
cruel words for the misguided use of
movie licences such as *Friday the
13th* and many others in the 1980s.
But this territory has been well
covered elsewhere, in Kevin Sullivan's
piece on *www.myvideogames.com*…

Better yet, I could really geek-out with
the details and highlight all of the games
that have guest-starred as cabinets
and screens inside movies. But
someone has beaten me to the punch.
Go to *www.mameworld.net/movies*
for the full story.

Then there is the whole *Tomb Raider,
Mortal Kombat, Pokémon, Final
Fantasy* game-to-film connection.
Does Hollywood really need to be so
literal? Certainly the language and
style of game media have had
tremendous influence on recent film
direction and camera movement, as
a broad selection of cinematic efforts
can attest: the style and bullets of
The Matrix, the bamboo groves and
airborne fight-dancing of *Crouching
Tiger, Hidden Dragon*, and the all-
seeing camera eye in the first scenes
of *Being John Malkovich*. The list goes
on. There is, in fact, a whole book
being written about the upcoming
persistent world of one of the globe's
most popular film and game breeding
grounds: *Star Wars Civilizations*.
Hollywood has certainly stood up and
taken notice of the new kid on the
cinematic block.

But while each of these topics would
offer a reasonable line of argument,
my interest lies elsewhere, in a
space hovering just under the current
radar of independent cinema. It is a
place where the practice of filmmaking
and the play of games collide, a place
that will be of increasing importance
in the years to come. This is the
little-known but fast-developing world
of Machinima.

'As boundaries between disciplines
collapse, new channels suggesting
thought and development open up.
The correspondence across these
once separated territories may not
follow purely "reasonable" lines.'
Steven Holl (*Intertwining*, Princeton
Architecural Press, 1996)

Under the Radar

Part theatre, part film, part videogame,
Machinima are animated movies
made utilizing the client-side, real-time
3D rendering technology of game
engines. From the ancient *Quake I*
to the tricky *Half-Life* or *Unreal
Tournament* engine, the technology
of the game code is giving shape to
a new form of storytelling born from
the culture of the first-person shooter
(FPS). In this digicinematic underworld,
gamers – hackers – filmmakers
conjure (and Quake) within virtual
environments, building sets and
moulding characters in an imaginary
world defined by a slightly disturbing
– still elementary – World-Wide
Wrestling Federation-meets-Philip K.
Dick aesthetic. It is the physics of a
strange universe recorded in pixels
per second distributed and consumed
via the web.

Top

Ranger Gone Bad 2
The Rangers
Quake I Engine

Bottom left

Eschaton: Nightfall
Strange Company
Quake II Engine

Bottom right

Devil's Covenant
Clan Phantasm
Quake I Engine

Int. computer screen – Scotland
Hugh Hancock, chairman of
Strange Company, an Edinburgh-
based organization devoted to the
advancement of filmmaking via
computer-generated media, writes:

Date: Fri, 26 Nov 1999 18:15:38
+0000
To: Katie Salen
From: Strange Company
Subject: Re: more Machinima

Clan Phantasm wrote their feature-
length film *Devil's Covenant* set in the
far future, with over 15 separate sets,
special effects and non-human characters
populating their world. It took them
a year to make, part-time, and cost
them nothing. Strange Company
Production's film, *Eschaton: Nightfall*,
is a near-future action nightmare set
in the Gigeresque world of H.P.
Lovecraft: to produce it on real film
would have cost us $1 million at a
conservative estimate, but in Machinima
we produced it for $300.

Added to that is the fact that
Machinima can then be distributed
over the Internet: *Nightfall* took
just three hours to download over
a normal modem, for 35 minutes of
full-screen, DVD-quality footage. The
same film would have taken close to
a month to download if it had been
in any conventional format. Added to
that is the speed at which Machinima
is advancing in quality, the fact that
with 'virtual cameras' you can develop
an entirely new language of film,
not hampered by the constraints of
the real world…

Movies produced within the culture
of first-person shooter games like
Quake, *Doom* and *Unreal* suggest
a model of moviemaking that may
challenge digital video's current
dominance by offering alternative
modes of representation and
distribution. Curiously, much of the
discussion surrounding the growth
of digital cinema has centred
on production issues: new tools and
lower budgets, etc. From an artistic
point of view, these factors are
significant, and movies made utilizing
game-engine technology certainly
look poised to contribute, despite
their status as an emerging cinematic
form. The area where this medium
might make the most impact,
however, is in the realm of online
distribution, an area that has received
little attention to date.

Currently, the main barrier to
distribution of digital cinema over
the Internet is the enormous
bandwidth requirements and the poor
quality that is achieved even when
these requirements are satisfied. The
Machinima scene, with its real-time
3D rendering capabilities and client-
side players (such as the Lithtech
Film Player developed by Strange
Company), seems to offer an
intriguing new model for animated
film production. Somewhere in the
intersection between the code of
the game engine, an elegant system
of distribution and the improvisation
of game play lies the raw material
of a filmic form waiting to explode.

Almost as soon as *Quake* was released
in 1996, gamers began to try and play
through its levels as fast as possible,
and to share recordings of their feats
with others, trying to beat each
other's times. This type of competition,
known as speedrunning, had been
established in the early days of
Doom, a game that like *Quake* gave
players the ability to record and save
their game play. Known as 'demos',
these recordings were used to publicize
a player or clan's playing prowess,
or were made to share information
on newly discovered tricks and cheats.
It was only a matter of time before
someone made the leap to movies.

According to *Quake* lore, in August
1996 a clan known as the Rangers
conceived the idea to record a
demo that would exploit the built-in
moviemaking capabilities of the
software. Rather than restrict their
demo recording to actual game play
– or to speedrunning – the Rangers
would use their *Quake* players as
actors, conceptually transforming the
game space into a virtual movie set.
As short and simple as the film
appears today – we see *Quake* bodies
walking around a deathmatch map,
pretending that they are in a movie;
text messages sent by the players
represent speech – *Diary of a Camper*
established a filmic genre that has
spawned hundreds of movies to date.
These movies range from less than a
minute to two hours in length, reference
genres from sci-fi fantasy to 1950s
sitcoms, and challenge the viewer to
rethink their assumptions about the
role of videogame technology in the
future of animated film.

While the formal language of Machinima has close ties to the games from which they are derived, the production process used in their creation closely mirrors that of other forms of digital filmmaking. From cameras to editing to the use of special effects (both real-time and post-produced), Machinima shares many of filmmaking's most basic tools and methodologies. Additionally, like film, Machinima engages questions about the role of specialized looking, or point of view. Recams, or demos of game play refilmed and edited from alternative perspectives and distributed as movies, clearly demonstrate the role point of view plays in affecting representation. The expertly recammed match between two of the world's top *Quake* players, Thresh and Billox, by Overman of Zarathustra Studios (*see www.planetquake.com/zs/recams/recams.html*), for example, not only allows viewers to experience the game play from a third-person perspective, but situates the viewer both literally and figuratively outside of the militarized language of *Quake* and other FPS games.

In contrast to filmic concerns such as transition, montage and characterization, the mode of seeing privileged by first-person shooters is one of positioning, tracking, identifying, predicting and targeting. This point of view, in which all modes of seeing are framed through a weapon's line of sight, reduces the space of play to that which is immediately accessible, visible and targetable. With the shift in perspective from first to third person offered by a recam, we are reminded of the profound difference between playing a deathmatch round of *Quake* and watching a recam of it. Recamming offers a point of transition between player and spectator, opening up the line of sight to include the possibility of the filmic eye.

Moreover, when a player utilizes the code of a game space in support of moviemaking, his or her double agency as player/actor serves to connect to two critical qualities of play: improvisation and performance. The inherent theatricality of Quakespace lends itself as a stage, albeit one most often dressed in industrial gloom and space-age weirdness. One group of Machinima producers has uniquely exploited the performative quality of FPS play, to great comedic effect. The ILL Clan (*www.illclan.com*), a New York City-based production team with roots in improvisational comedy, entered the Machinima scene with the release of their first film, *Apartment Huntin'*. The film tells the story of Lenny and Larry, two bumbling lumberjacks on a mission to rent an apartment.

Recognizing that the process of making a *Quake* movie was more akin to virtual puppeteering than method acting, the group initially embraced the limitations of the technology by utilizing props and characters native to Quakespace, opting to allow the narrative to develop in real time, through improvisation. Thus, the native weapons of Quake – guns and axes – were transformed into tools of the trade for the story's two lumberjacks.

Opposite page top

Rendezvous
Nanoflix
Quake II **Engine**

Opposite page bottom and this page

Blahbalicious
Avatar and Wendigo
Quake I **Engine**

Int. computer screen – New York ILL Clinton, member of the ILL Clan, writes:

Date: Thu, 18 Nov 1999 19:09:13 +0500
To: Katie Salen
From: ILL Clan movie method
Subject: Re:

Our writing technique was inspired by Chuck Jones (the guy who practically created Bugs Bunny) in his book *Chuck Amuck*. We start with a theme… like two guys looking for an apartment. We then come up with something Chuck Jones calls 'business', basically just a bunch of silly things that happen around an established theme, rather than developing a storyline or plot. In our case, this meant making a list of silly things that could happen in a *Quake* map.

Once we had very loose storyboards, we went to an LAN (Local Area Network) where we could all sit in front of separate machines, but still see and hear one another. This is really important. I heard that the Rangers made their demo by collaborating over the net. I can't even imagine trying to do that! You see, we improvise all of the dialogue – if we couldn't see or hear each other it wouldn't have worked. Improv is our basic working method. I'm an improv performer and ILL Bixby and ILL Robinson have both taken improv classes. The three of us used to do improv together on an online show called *Metaplay* (now defunct). The show took place in a graphical chatroom where we developed performances based on the online audience's suggestions. But I digress… where were we? Oh, we sat together in an LAN.

ILL Bixby operated the camera, and ILL Smith, ILL Robinson and I were the characters. We blocked it all out, which is film-speak for deciding where you stand, and then we'd run through it and make up dialogue as we went. ILL Bixby is a grip in real life, and I've worked on film sets too, and let me tell you, this was EXACTLY like making a movie on a real set, except we were all in front of computers. But it felt exactly the same.

The ILL Clan's newest film, *Hardly Workin'* – the most visually and conceptually sophisticated Machinima film to date – combines this improvisational methodology with stunning visual design. Rather than using the maps and models of the game as they had done in their first film, the ILL Clan created 99 per cent of their own game assets for *Hardly Workin'*, combining the look and feel of cartoons with FPS technology. While telling a good story is never simple – particularly when the filmmaker must combine the talents of a writer, coder, director and animator – the innovative work of the ILL Clan suggests that good stories are always possible.

It is important to note, however, that 'acting' in a *Quake* movie is neither instinctual, nor particularly easy. Game engines accommodate a limited set of physical gestures (again, they are designed for fast-paced, kill-or-be-killed movement) and, despite the immersive qualities of the virtual acting environment, the physical separation between the actor and his onscreen representation poses certain problems, point of view and timing being just two of them.

Additionally, and perhaps most importantly, the form of stylized interaction required of 'acting' is quite different from that required of 'playing'. The stylized play of *Quake* and other first-person shooters is context-specific, as are all forms of game play. Players behave quite differently in Quakespace than they do in the land of *Myst*; behaviour is simultaneously technology-dependent and spatially determined. The result is that it can be very difficult to overcome the ergonomic and contextual prejudice of the first-person shooter environment. Not surprisingly, the genre's most successful films are those that recognize and embrace these limitations (films like Nanoflix's *Rendezvous*, Zarathustra Studio's *Father Frags Best*, and Avatar and Wendigo's *Blahbalicious*, for example).

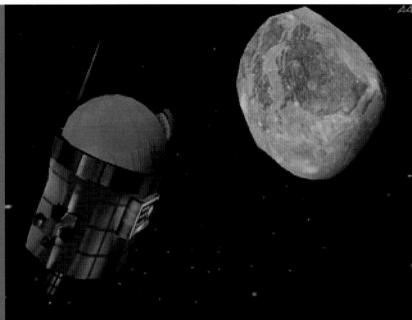

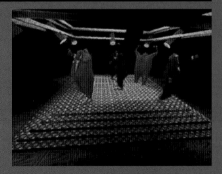

**Quake III Arena
Trailer
Pre-rendered
Cinematics**

*Int. computer screen – Gamers.com
Anna Kang, founder of Fountainhead
Entertainment:*

Machinima's the new kid on the block
so it has yet to prove itself. If game
technology moves forward at the
pace I believe it will, Machinima will
revolutionize animation. Like CGI,
Machinima will have a place in
animation history. We will have CGI,
stop motion, claymation, anime and
Machinima as the primary styles
of creating animated features if you're
not into traditional cell animation.

To get there, however, a Machinima
project will need to go beyond the
hobbyist level. It will need a compelling
story with unique media that will
entertain and absorb the audience.
(from: gamers.com, interview)

Strange universe

In her essay 'The Scene of the Screen',
Vivian Sobchack suggests that some
major cultural changes can be seen as
'directly inspired by new technology',
while others occur relatively
independently, and others still
emerge from the new 'technological
metaphors and analogies' that
indirectly alter the structures of
perceptual life and thought (*Materialities
of Communication*, Stanford University
Press, 1994). Arguably, the implications
of videogame technology go far
beyond a contribution to the field
of animated film. Cognitive scientists,
philosophers and psychologists, to
name but a few, are busy exploring the
changes evoked by electronic culture.
Machinima, too, despite its relative
youth, seems poised to contribute to
this discussion via its inventive reuse
of game-engine technology.

One additional channel of development
lies in the application of modern 3D
game technology to contexts outside
of game design. Leaders in VR
development, for instance, have found
game engines to have broad appeal.
Bob Barry, a VR researcher currently
working with Epic Games' *Unreal*
engine, writes, 'The benefits of using
a game engine outside of the gaming
world are clear. The most obvious
benefit is the incredible reduction in
development costs when moving
away from the SGI platform. Other
benefits include cross-platform
support, low requirements for end-
user hardware, industry and community
support, and development hardware
and software support. Moreover, we
have seen a trend in the gaming
industry that enables users to extend
the gaming environment via scripting
languages, terrain editors, world
builders, etc. Because of the
extendibility, users are more apt to
stay with a particular game for longer
periods of time, allowing larger
communities to develop. The original
Quake community is one of the best
examples of this as it rests on an
engine that is almost two generations
old, yet is still strong and growing
to this day.' Animated film appears to
be only the first of many territories
upon which the strange universe
of Machinima may ultimately have
an impact.

Katie Salen

Fade to black.

So far, not as much has been made of the potential for new filmic language in Machinima. Certainly, Machinima films have, with a few exceptions, stuck to the conventional techniques of film, without exploring the new options that CGI and Machinima give the filmmaker. Here is Strange Company's list of 10 critical elements of Machinima:

1 Viewer Control

Machinima, alone of any filmic medium, allows viewers to have a nearly unlimited level of control over their viewing angle and position. Imagine *The Blair Witch Project*, where the viewer is looking around and following the action himself, as panicked as the characters; or a *Twin Peaks*-like murder mystery, where the viewer can wander around the town of his own free will, trying to piece together the parts of the story.

2 Set as Chessboard

The possibilities for Machinima dialogue aren't just limited to the camera. Rather than having a transition between scenes as a post-produced 2D effect on the image on screen, the transition can be 3D, with the set and characters falling into pieces like a jigsaw, sliding off-screen like the set of a Broadway musical, or going up in a puff of smoke to reveal a new scene.

3 Walk Through Walls

In *Citizen Kane*, Orson Welles spent an inordinate amount of time and money on a single camera shot, where the camera appears to move seamlessly through a glass window. Without the annoying restrictions of reality and physics, in Machinima the viewpoint can be anywhere.

4 Morphing Transitions

Whilst morphing is an established filmic technique, the sheer ease of morphing between computer-generated images allows filmmakers to use it in a whole new way. Rather than just using a morph as a complex and literal special effect (à la *Terminator 2*), entire scenes and shots can morph into one another, allowing the filmmaker to use a morph as a scene transition in much the same way a conventional filmmaker would use a wipe or a dissolve.

5 Line Of Sight

Have you ever noticed how any first-person perspective shot in a film always looks slightly wrong? The reason for this problem in simple: a human's point of focus, the object on which they are concentrating their attention, changes too fast for any human cameraman to be able to simulate the movement, particularly given that said human's point of focus changes just as quickly. Machinima can easily simulate human eye movement, however, focusing the camera on an invisible target that moves around the set as the 'eye's' focus changes.

6 Depth Of Field

With the Voodoo 4 coming soon, Machinima will be able to simulate depth of field, something that has been missing until now. However, the fact that it will be simulated opens up many possibilities for the filmmaker. Depths of field can be altered, changing from a normal sharp focus on one point all the way to a total absence of depth of field, where objects in the extreme foreground are as sharp as those in the distance.

7 Extreme Close-up!

Whilst conventional filmmakers have a good deal of control over their Field Of View, the Machinima creator has more. Machinima can use any field of view, from a tiny ultra-close up (beloved of filmmakers like David Lynch, for instance), to an FOV of 180 degrees or more – even 360-degree panoramic vision. Such drastic changes in FOV could be used, again, for transitions, for bizarre pans (zooming out to 360-degree FOV, then in again to an object which was behind the camera), and more.

8 Is it Dark in Here?

Machinima also has total control over the lighting in a scene (within the constraints of dynamic lighting in current engines). Whilst simple effects, like dimming the lights in a room to total darkness, are obvious, Machinima offers many more possibilities. For example, consider a disembodied light, or flock of such lights, moving around the set, casting a glow without any physical component. Such lights could be used to highlight actors' faces at key points, pick out members of a crowd, or merely give a scene an unearthly ambience.

9 Duck!

The virtual nature of the camera in Machinima means that the filmmaker can send it where no sane cameraman would dare to go. In *Eschaton: Nightfall*, for example, the camera flew through the blades of a moving helicopter and between combatants in a hand-to-hand battle. This opens up the possibility for entirely new styles of action sequence, with longer, moving camera shots that can get closer to the action than would be possible with conventional methods.

10 Rendering Effects

Lastly, the mechanisms of rendering, used by Machinima to simulate reality, can also be used to achieve some truly unique results. Characters can become slightly lighter or darker than their surroundings, enabling the filmmaker to highlight them or suggest elements of their role. Any object can become more or less 'real', losing bump-mapping, shadowing; becoming transparent or translucent.

Tommy Pallotta, Ben Davis,
Casey Charvet, Anthony Bailey,
'Lord' Rev. Dr Paul Soth, Phil Rice
(aka Overman), Paul Steed,
id Software, Anders Carlsson
(aka Sip-Ice), United Recammers,
Matt Dominianni (aka ILL Clinton),
Paul Marino (aka ILL Robinson),
Joe Goss, Bryan Henderson (aka
Crustar), Jordan Crandall.

clan: a term for a group of players who practise and compete together on a regular basis within the culture of *Quake* and other first-person shooter games. Every clan gives itself a name, and members of that clan will add a two- or three-letter abbreviation as a tag to their own name to show membership in the clan. Like track and field, clans compete together in both solo and group events. Top clans are ranked and recognized like top players.

coder: someone with programming skills. In the case of *Quake* movies, coders are the ones who add in various special effects and other modifications to the game for the film. Coders are also the people who make editing software for the games, such as file extractors, modelling software and recamming software.

deathmatch: see co-op, CTF (capture the flag) and Team Deathmatch. A multi-player mode where two or more players compete to get the most kills, commonly referred to as 'frags'. In a deathmatch, the only way to get points is to kill other players.

demos: a recording of play within a game space. See taxonomy of a demo. A somewhat lost art form once used by young programmers to demonstrate their skill in modelling, graphics and mastery of programming.

frag: to kill.

game engine: the main layer of software in a game; the heart of the game. The engine is responsible for setting up the environment and it generally contains sub-parts such as the rendering engine, the game's physical properties, the user IO and the game's interactivity. Parts of the engine may be modified or swapped without having to reprogram everything. Just as several different models of a Honda may contain the same engine, several different games can be based on the same engine.

LAN: Local Area Network; a high-speed data connection. LANs are important to multi-player gaming because they offer the fastest possible interconnection to the players. Also related to low ping times and low lag.

Machinima: the emergent filmic medium of client-side, real-time generated 3D computer animation, of which *Quake* movies are one example.

mods: a modification to the game that results in a change in the format of game play.

movies: movies are simply demos which are recorded using actors, a plot, a camera and a set rather than a record of a person's playing. Usually they are made from several demos put together using a demo editor such as Film@11 or Keygrip.

recammer: someone who uses a programme called a Demo Editor to take a game demo (usually a demo recording of the final match of a tournament or other important game) to add in camera effects, music and other additions.

recams: a movie product of recammers.

speed runners: players who specialize in finishing a game in record fast times. In the case of *Quake* movies, their speed runs are recorded and recammed.

taxonomy of a demo:
a. Game demo: recording of a match, tournament, or fragfest.
b. Speedrunning demos: there are two distinct kinds: 100 per cent demos (those in which the player kills all the monsters and finds all the secrets), and runs (those in which the sole purpose is to finish the level, caring only for time, not for kills or secrets).
c. Recams: a game demo to which camera effects, music and other production effects are added.
d. Movies: demos recorded using actors, a plot, a camera and a set.

Myst was probably one of the first really deeply narrative games to make a big splash. The reason for this is that it was based on a fundamental quality of play: discovery.

The notion of narrative in videogames has become somewhat controversial among theorists these days. Let me clarify. There doesn't seem to be much disagreement among 'indigenous' theorists, that is, those of us primarily engaged in studying games. However, theorists from other disciplines seem to be wildly divergent in their opinions about the role, or lack thereof, of narrative in games. This is a direct result of theoretical 'repurposing'. Traditionally, repurposing is viewed as an intermediate evolutionary step in the development of any new communications medium, and it frequently yields mutant life forms that don't quite hit the mark.

Among those I consider to be 'true' game theorists, that is, people who are game-centric in their theoretical ideas, there are different approaches, but few substantive disagreements. In general, we tend to look at game narrative 'on its own terms'. Although we compare videogames to other media, we are extremely clear on the fact that they have unique and distinctive properties that differentiate them from other expressive forms.

In studying games and trying to understand their value as a form of cultural production, it's crucial to recognize that games are fundamentally about play, so a play-centric framework is needed in order to look at the function of narrativity in games. I started looking at these issues while working on a project for the sector of the game industry that is now called 'out-of-home' or 'location-based' entertainment (LBE), for New York-based Edwin Schlossberg Incorporated. Over a period that spanned 1983 to 1989, we tried to develop network games designed to facilitate positive social interaction. They were networked (which was some feat when we started, since PCs were not yet typically networkable), integrated both co-operation and competition, and were specifically designed for adults with a high priority on gender neutrality. Violence was banned, and all the games had some kind of narrative layer to contextualize them in the overall venue, which was loosely themed around the idea of a city.

Having had no previous experience with games (indeed, when I started there were no professional game designers on staff, although this later changed), I embarked on an extensive research project to deconstruct games and find out 'what they were made of'. In order to create a set of standard criteria for our products, I studied literally dozens of games, from board games to arcade and videogames. What I ultimately identified was a basic definition that included six features that all games shared.

A game is a structured framework for spontaneous play consisting of:

– A goal (and a variety of related sub-goals)
– Obstacles (designed to prevent you from obtaining your goal)
– Resources (to assist you in obtaining your goal)
– Rewards (for progress in the game, often in the form of resources)
– Penalties (for failing to overcome obstacles, often in the form of more obstacles)
– Information
  – Known to all players and the game
  – Known to individual players (e.g., a hand of cards)
  – Known only to the game
  – Progressive information (moves from one state of knowledge to another, e.g. Chance cards in Monopoly)

Cyan's *Myst* immerses players in an enigmatic story world

STORY AS PLAY SPACE

One of the common factors of all the games we were working on was that they all had some kind of narrative. For instance, one was about helping to restore power to a city undergoing a blackout, another was a stockbroker role-playing game, etc. In each case, the narrative was clearly identified as having the function of an interface metaphor. This was about two years before the Macintosh interface hit the market, so we were still living in 'DOSland'. But like many pioneers before us, we realized that people could relate to computers more easily through metaphors, and we were particularly interested in using narrative metaphors. We wanted people to feel as though they were inside these little mini-stories, which were ultimately theirs to play around with and direct. Our ideas were very ambitious, so much so that they were never actually implemented, although many companies that later went on to implement LBE projects saw our prototypes early on.

**Opposite page
and this page top,
bottom right**

*Indiana Jones
and the
Infernal Machine*

Bottom left

Virtual Adventures
(creative director:
Celia Pearce; Iwerks
Entertainment and
Evans & Sutherland)
attempted to
merge story, game
and virtual reality.

What's interesting about the framework described above is that it also maps very nicely onto narrative structure, something that was articulated in 1993 when I developed another LBE game, *Virtual Adventures: The Loch Ness Expedition* for Iwerks Entertainment and Evans & Sutherland. As creative director for this high-end virtual-reality game, it was very clear to both myself and the rest of the team that we could create a really compelling narrative using this technology, even though we only had three minutes to do it in. The experience was a 24-player mission in which four teams of six 'scientists' were sent to the bottom of Loch Ness in submersibles to rescue Nessie's eggs from bounty hunters. (Actually, through the trickery of VR, we were able to make each team look like good guys to themselves and bad guys to everyone else.)

One of the things that was happening at this point was that filmmakers, who had previously all but ignored if not deplored videogames, were suddenly stormtrooping our little nerddom, deciding that they were going to apply their brilliant storytelling talent to our silly medium. This attempt at repurposing, which at its worst was something that came to be dubbed 'shovelware', had at best mixed results. Successful attempts included the *Indiana Jones* games, which were really smart because they were based on a story that was already a game. Less successful attempts included *Voyeur*, which, though hyped as an early CDI 'interactive movie', at the end of the day was not as captivating as its peeping-Tom premise suggested it might be. Generally speaking, 'non-linear' stories and 'interactive cinema' have proved to be a faulty premise at best. The reason for this is that they have everything but the one thing that a good game needs: play. When you remove play from the equation, all you have is an author giving you permission to do some minor tinkering with a linear story. Exploring various branching paths is less than enthralling. Video as a medium is inherently linear. As soon as the video starts, the interactivity goes away. Furthermore, it is almost impossible to match the production, acting and writing quality of film in a CD-ROM. Misguided attempts to do so have yielded such eminently unmemorable experiences as the *Johnny Mnemonic* game, whose mediocrity was rivalled only by the film on which it was based.

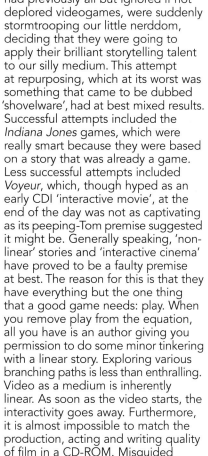

Myst was probably one of the first really deeply narrative games to make a big splash. The reason for this is that it was based on a fundamental quality of play: discovery. While the story itself was fairly linear (that is, you couldn't really change the course of events until the very end), it was the process of constructing the story in your head that made the game compelling. *Myst* – as well as its sequels – is like a treasure hunt in that regard, which is really its genius.
It is also based on the unspoken but inherent implication that the player is smart. This is one of the things that draws people into these sorts of games. Game players do not like to be spoon-fed their narrative. They like to uncover it at their own pace. And the longer it takes, and the harder it is, the better. Because if they succeed, they feel that much smarter for having done so.

To really ponder the value of narrative play, think about some of the typical things you did as a kid. Aren't *Quake* and *Half-Life* just more high-tech versions of cops and robbers? Aren't Massively Multi-player Online Role Playing Games (MMORPGs) just an elaborate form of that old favourite, dressing-up? And isn't *Crazy Taxi* just a modern-day version of *Hot Wheels*? Will Wright of Maxis describes his own games in such terms. *Sim City* is a model railroad, while *The Sims* is a doll's house. At the core of these games are fundamental paradigms of play which appear to be fairly universal. Battle simulations, role-play, constructing miniature towns, 'playing house' can all be seen in various forms in many different countries. Toy cars are popular even in African villages, where children construct them from wire hangers to navigate around the neighbourhood.

This page top left, bottom left, centre

The Sims

This page bottom right

MMORPG game Ultima Online creates a social narrative experience

Opposite page top

Games like *Everquest* **are peopled with magical characters and monsters**

Opposite page bottom

Riven

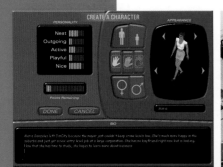

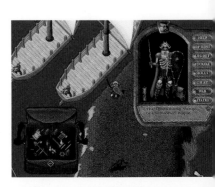

Board games follow a similar pattern. Chess demonstrates some of the fundamental differences between storytelling and story-making, which is a good way to distinguish play-based narrative from other forms. The narrative in chess is abstracted and metaphorical, allowing the player to project his or her own character onto the pieces. In fact, as a rule, game characters tend to be less articulated (or, in the case of *Myst*, not articulated at all), for the very reason that they allow for this level of projection or displacement. You can see this clearly in a game like *Indiana Jones*; the character is far less articulated than in the movie, functioning as a sort of digital action figure that allows the player to imagine him- or herself as Indy. Games that tend to have highly articulated characters are seldom successful. The more the author controls the character, the less the player does. The trick is in coming up with the right balance. One of my favourite examples of this is the game *Blade Runner*, by Westwood Studios. When you begin the game, it is not determined whether your character, a Blade Runner whose mission is to capture renegade replicants, is a human or a replicant himself. However, the game watches what you do to determine which you believe yourself to be. At some point, it makes an assessment based on your actions, then sends the story on the appropriate trajectory. This is a great example of optimizing the computer's capability. It constructs the story around you, creating a totally customized experience. In this way, the narrative is playing with you.

This idea of a deconstructed narrative, that is, breaking down the essential ingredients of a story, helps us to understand how narrative operates in games. Leaving much up to the imagination and action of the player is tough for typical practitioners of other narrative media. It forces them to give up a certain amount of control, which really goes against their training.

I like to look at the whole story/game relationship in terms of 'narrative operators', each of which has a role to play in creating a narrative or story-like experience. It is important to realize, however, that all of these operators function in the service of play, which is the heart and soul of what games are about. 'Emergent' here means something that is not predetermined, but that evolves over time out of a rule-based system. As the examples given demonstrate, most games include combinations of one or more of these six narrative operators.

– Experiential. The emergent narrative that arises out of the game 'conflict' as it is played out, as experienced by the players themselves. In sports, for example, the game narrative from the players' point of view.
– Performative. The emergent narrative as seen by spectators watching and/or interpreting the game underway. In sports, the game as experienced by the stadium or television audience, and retold by the commentators.
– Augmentary. Layers of information, interpretation, background and contextual frameworks around the game that enhance other narrative operators. In sports, this includes pre- and post-game analysis, scores and stats, background, player and coach interviews, and other elements that augment the game in progress.
– Descriptive. The retelling of game events to third parties, and the culture that emerges out of that. In terms of sports, an entire section of the newspaper is devoted to this.
– Meta-story. A specific narrative 'overlay' or narrative metaphor that contextualizes the game rules. In sports, there is no meta-story. However, in chess for example, the meta-story is a battle between two kingdoms; in *Monopoly* it is a contest between capitalist land barons.
– Story system. A rule-based story system or kit of generic narrative parts that allows players to create their own characters and story, such as is the case with *The Sims*. Story systems can exist independently of or in conjunction with a meta-story, such as with *Dungeons and Dragons* or MMORPGs.

Opposite page

Medieval chess set in the Tower of London

This page

Blade Runner

Using this approach really helps us to better understand the function of narrative in play and therefore in games. The key is in letting go of the notion of games as interactive story-telling and trying to engage players in a more pro-active relationship with the narrative.

If current trends continue, and the story genres they encompass continue to grow broader and more diversified, immersive play-based narrative experiences are going to become the most popular form of mass-medium narrative. Game designers will come up with increasingly interesting and compelling forms of narrative play, which take advantage of the procedural aspects of computing to engage the player's imagination and creativity in ever more dynamic ways.

Celia Pearce

ERIC ZIMMERMAN

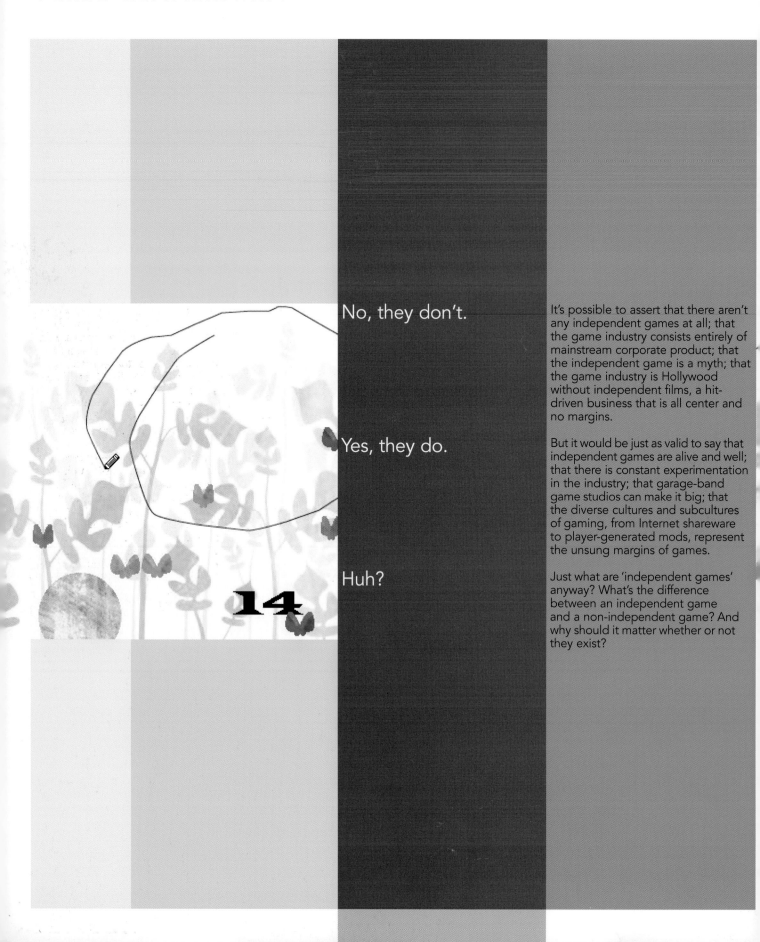

No, they don't.

Yes, they do.

Huh?

14

It's possible to assert that there aren't any independent games at all; that the game industry consists entirely of mainstream corporate product; that the independent game is a myth; that the game industry is Hollywood without independent films, a hit-driven business that is all center and no margins.

But it would be just as valid to say that independent games are alive and well; that there is constant experimentation in the industry; that garage-band game studios can make it big; that the diverse cultures and subcultures of gaming, from Internet shareware to player-generated mods, represent the unsung margins of games.

Just what are 'independent games' anyway? What's the difference between an independent game and a non-independent game? And why should it matter whether or not they exist?

Before we dig down into these questions, let's take a brief sideways glance at cinema, a medium where the concept of the independent product seems to be indisputably alive and well. 'Independent film' is a term that the critics, creators and viewers of films all seem quite comfortable using. So how do they differentiate an independent movie from one that isn't?

1 Independence can refer to the way in which a film is funded, marketed and distributed. Was it a studio production? Or was it financed from a grant? And where can the film be seen? In a corporate multiplex or in an alternative art house?

2 It can also have to do with the film medium itself. Was it a short or a feature? Was the scope of production a shoestring budget or a multimillion dollar extravaganza?

3 Lastly, the idea of independence in film can refer to something more vague, to the overall spirit and culture of the film. Is it the usual Hollywood formula, or do the storyline and cinematography somehow question mainstream filmmaking?

Independence in cinema is associated with the economic, technological or cultural qualities of a film. The possibility of independent games can also be plotted in terms of these three overlapping vectors. If independent games do exist, then they're independent because something about their economic, technological or cultural status makes them so.

The initial question remains: do independent games exist? But is it really a yes or no question? If it is, I'm not ready to come down on one side or the other just yet. I'd rather be able to speak out of both sides of my mouth. And so, as I take a look at the economic, technological and cultural factors that contribute to the answer, I'll be keeping a running dialogue with myself. Pick your favorite column.

C5 L5

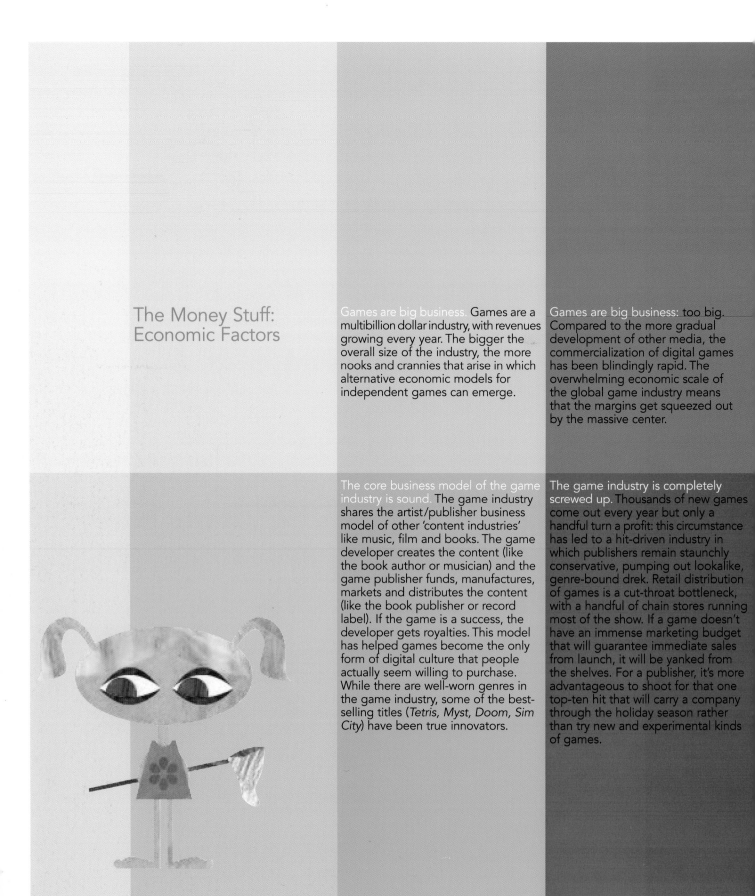

The Money Stuff:
Economic Factors

Games are big business. Games are a multibillion dollar industry, with revenues growing every year. The bigger the overall size of the industry, the more nooks and crannies that arise in which alternative economic models for independent games can emerge.

Games are big business: too big. Compared to the more gradual development of other media, the commercialization of digital games has been blindingly rapid. The overwhelming economic scale of the global game industry means that the margins get squeezed out by the massive center.

The core business model of the game industry is sound. The game industry shares the artist/publisher business model of other 'content industries' like music, film and books. The game developer creates the content (like the book author or musician) and the game publisher funds, manufactures, markets and distributes the content (like the book publisher or record label). If the game is a success, the developer gets royalties. This model has helped games become the only form of digital culture that people actually seem willing to purchase. While there are well-worn genres in the game industry, some of the best-selling titles (*Tetris, Myst, Doom, Sim City*) have been true innovators.

The game industry is completely screwed up. Thousands of new games come out every year but only a handful turn a profit: this circumstance has led to a hit-driven industry in which publishers remain staunchly conservative, pumping out lookalike, genre-bound drek. Retail distribution of games is a cut-throat bottleneck, with a handful of chain stores running most of the show. If a game doesn't have an immense marketing budget that will guarantee immediate sales from launch, it will be yanked from the shelves. For a publisher, it's more advantageous to shoot for that one top-ten hit that will carry a company through the holiday season rather than try new and experimental kinds of games.

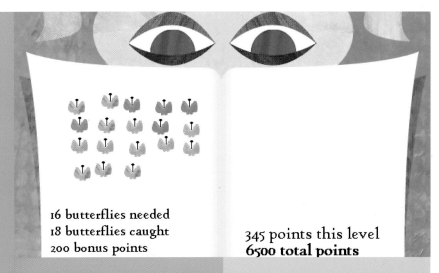

16 butterflies needed
18 butterflies caught
200 bonus points

345 points this level
6500 total points

The Internet will make independent games possible. In the future, game consumers will be able to purchase games online directly from developers, downloading data instead of buying a manufactured disk or cartridge. This encourages independent games by eliminating the distribution snafu: players can choose any game they like instead of being limited to the mainstream titles that retailers choose to put on store shelves.

Nobody knows how to make money online. The shareware business model, in which players download a free game demo and pay for the full version of the game, has rarely proved lucrative. CD-ROM games are often hundreds of megabytes of data, meaning hours of download time for most computer users. The Internet economy, including online gaming sites, seems to be in a complete shambles.

Other media have alternative contexts for production, distribution and reception. As the game industry matures, the equivalent of small record labels, college radio stations and experimental DJs will come into their own.

It's a chicken-and-egg situation. These 'alternative contexts' will come into being only when the game industry undergoes a number of major paradigm shifts in the ways that games are produced, distributed and played. These shifts are unlikely to happen before the games themselves change.

This page and opposite page
Loop

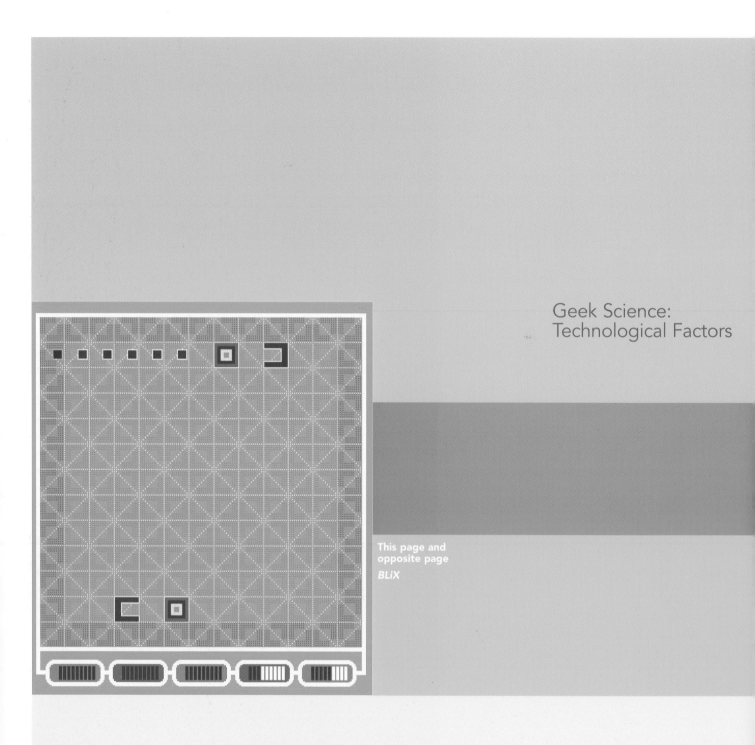

Geek Science:
Technological Factors

**This page and
opposite page**
BLiX

The technology is getting better. There's no other cultural medium that, like games, reinvents its own technical capabilities every few years. New game technologies mean more depth, more complexity and more ways to play. Technology drives innovation.

Technology is overemphasized. The game industry is completely technofetishistic, with the value of games typically being judged on their technical merits. Innovation in games needs to come from sources other than hardware and software technology.

Games are bigger than ever. No longer the product of a single programmer, games are substantial undertakings requiring the kind of creative, multi-stage, interdisciplinary collaboration found in film. The increase of professional standards in regard to scope and process is a necessary step in the maturation of the medium.

Games are bigger than ever. As games get bigger, they get more expensive. And the most expensive games set the standard for production values in all games. Games are complicated to produce and low-fi approaches are frowned upon. It's possible for a band to record an album in a garage over a weekend. But not so with games.

New game platforms keep the industry on its toes. The constant competition between the major industry players means that games will always be maximizing the latest capabilities of PCs and that new consoles will appear on the market every year or two. Games must rise to meet these ever-changing technological needs and the result is a lack of stagnation in the games themselves.

The industry indulges in planned obsolescence. Platform follows platform like the emperor's new clothes. In contrast to the more universal formats of the videotape or audio CD, the resulting plethora of standards makes archiving and playing older games a hobbyist's trade. The result is a medium without a history, in which technical innovation becomes an end, not a means.

Games are merging with cinema. Technological advances, particularly in real-time graphics, mean that games are becoming more 'realistic' and increasingly resemble film. The cinematic turn in games will allow developers a broader palette of expressive tools that will appeal to new kinds of game audiences. Games will absorb and replace film.

Games suffer from cinema envy. What passes for 'realism' in games is an awkward and unimaginative use of 3D computer graphics. It's time for game developers to stop trying to replicate the pleasures of film. Games need to find their own forms of expression, capitalizing on their unique properties as dynamic, participatory systems.

The Little Boys' Club: Cultural Factors

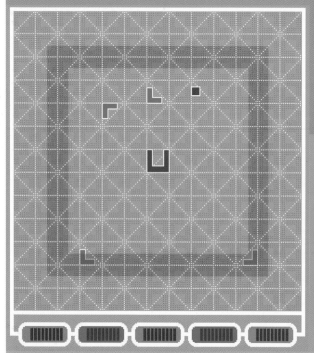

Game developers care about their work. With lower average salaries than the rest of the software development industry, game developers make games because they love what they do. The game-development community is fiercely dedicated to the craft of making games and almost universally disgruntled with the homogeneous nature of the game industry. With these attitudes, breakout independent games are inevitable.

Games are made by and for hardcore gamers. Until this cycle is broken, games will remain stuck where they are culturally. Game developers are unapologetically geeky, blatantly anti-intellectual, and hostile to new ways of thinking about what they do. There are no established critical methodologies for game design and without ways of thinking outside the box, independent games are doomed.

Games are diversifying. Games are no longer the domain of young males. For example, the girls games movement made great strides in opening up new audiences for games. The Internet has introduced gaming to an older, multicultural audience of both genders. An increasingly 'interactive' society will demand interactive entertainment and, as the cultural credibility of games improves, they will replace other media to become the dominant leisure activity of our wired society.

The more things change, the more they stay the same. The legacy of the girls game movement isn't experimental independent games: it is Barbie CD-ROMs. Games, like comic books in the US, will never shed the stigma of being power fantasies for adolescent boys. Despite the incrementally diversifying audience for gaming, it is naïve to think that games will ever usurp film and television as the dominant form of entertainment.

This page and opposite page
BLiX

Games are influential pop culture. Fine artists are appropriating the imagery of videogames. DJs are sampling game audio effects. Videogame characters feature on Urban Outfitter T-shirts. PlayStations have been a mainstay of London clubs for years. This kind of hybrid appropriation is how healthy and robust media operate and is the proof of the relevance of games in culture at large. Game soundtracks feature tracks from hot DJs. Independent games will emerge from the intersection of games with music, fashion and other forms of culture.

It's a one-way street. It is true that games are being appropriated by other forms of culture. But the reverse just isn't true. The aesthetics and narratives of games are almost completely genre-bound. Game design and development needs to be seen as a cultural activity. This means, among other things, the development of a critical discourse that can bridge the theory and practice of games and help developers understand their work both as a disciplinary activity and, in broader terms, as the production of culture. Games should appropriate from a broader array of cultural sources. Forget D&D: how about Cubism or Hitchcock?

Game subcultures are thriving. From user-created game levels and avatars to grass-roots online game fan communities to the cultures of hacks and mods, the subcultures of games are incredibly rich. So stop complaining: independent games are already here.

There's a difference between fan culture and independent games. Game subcultures are composed of hardcore gamers and are focused inwards, on their own communities, rather than being concerned with changing the face of gaming culture at large. A true independent games movement will be something entirely different.

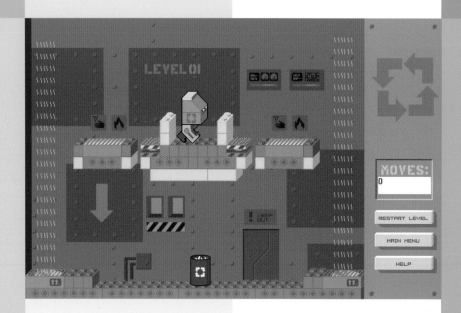

Opposite page
Junkbot

This page top
Junkbot

This page bottom
gameLab crew
from left

Peter Lee
Eric Zimmerman
Frank Lantz
Nick Fortugno
Peter Nicolai
Ranjit Bhatnagar
Tiko (the dog)

Pop culture is an ecosystem. Music and fashion; film and graphic design; television and manga. In diverse economies of scale, pop media network globally and locally, influencing each other in every sphere of society. Do digital games take part in this worldwide dance of culture?

Of course they do – but somehow only as a geeky cousin, twice removed from the family of other, hipper pop media. Or perhaps I'm being too hard on games, unfairly stereotyping them without appreciating their subtlety. Maybe games are part and parcel of the landscape of pop – but as with all new forms of media, their introduction into the mix redefines the way we have to consider the whole.

I'm crossing my fingers that the oh-so-young medium of digital games has many wonderful surprises in store for us, ways of constructing our lives and commenting on them that we have yet to experience. My hope is that games can offer radically new forms of culture, forms that are uniquely suited to the complex emergent systems which increasingly seem to constitute our understandings of the world.

The immediate question remains, however. The question that started this essay: do independent games exist or not? You've heard from both sides of my mouth. So which voice makes sense to you? Which column seemed to speak the truth – the left or the right? Actually, the two columns aren't intended as two separate answers. They're more like two related arguments. Or perhaps they're two halves of the same argument.

Do you want to know what I really think?

If you're a tourist to this world, someone outside the game industry, someone who doesn't play many games but is drawn to their glittering surfaces and wants to know more, read down the left. Appreciate games. Look beyond the shoot-'em-up stigma and try to see digital gaming as the deliciously complex and groundbreaking phenomenon that it is.

On the other hand, if you're not just a tourist, if you're already in the belly of the beast, if you're a game player, a game critic or even (can it be?) a game developer, read the right-hand column. Be disgruntled. Be dissatisfied. Demand more. Get angry with the state of things. Start a revolution. Do you need a place to begin? How about this: solve the unsolved problem of independent games.

If you don't, who will?

Eric Zimmerman

HEAD GAMES

         (1)   PLAY   (2)
     0000   0000   0000
MARK PESCE THE FUTURE OF PLAY

Of all the revolutions kindled by the personal computer, electronic gaming faces the brightest future. Consider this: 3D computer graphics, the essence of simulation and the core of modern videogaming, will be a trillion times faster in 2020 than they are today. Every five years, we get a thousand-fold speed improvement, with no end in sight. The photorealism of movies like *Shrek* or *Final Fantasy: The Spirits Within* will soon look as antique as the Atari 2600 does to us. In the future that awaits us, it will be completely impossible to distinguish between a computer-generated image and a live one. Most people will have given up trying – to the great consternation of TV news producers.

The boundaries between the real world and the imaginary realm of electronic play have already begun to blur; today's sports videogames look more and more like poorly lit TV broadcasts, and, at some point in the next five years, a parent is going to walk past a television set wondering, 'Is that live – or simulation?' Only the presence of game controllers, in the hands of the viewers, will give the answer away.

The boundaries between the real world and the imaginary realm of electronic play have already begun to blur.

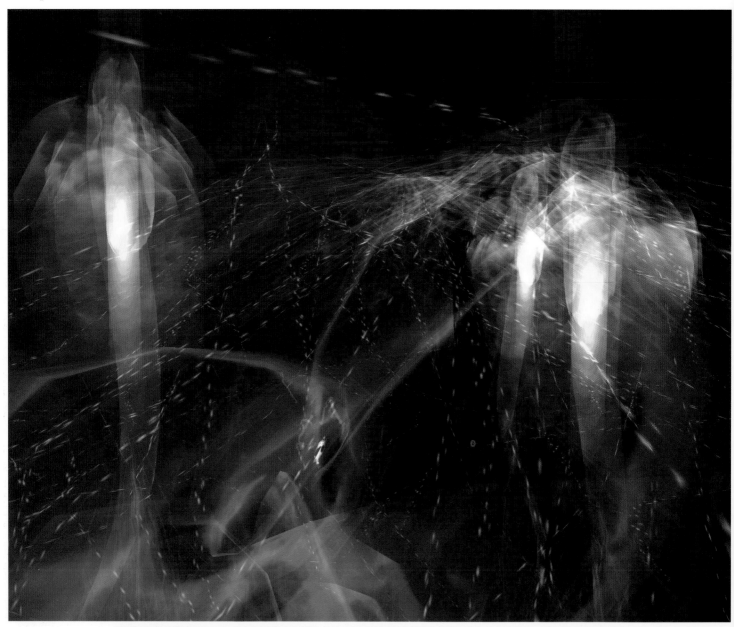

✳HEAD GAMES✳

As our computers approach outrageous speeds – and Moore's Law keeps doubling their performance every 18 months – we're coming to understand that it isn't just prettily rendered synthetic images that make a good game. In fact, the images may have little to do with it. Canadian artist Char Davies has produced two interactive works, *Osmose* (1995) and *Ephemere* (1998), that use quarter-million-dollar supercomputers and fully encompassing sensory gear – the head-mounted display of virtual reality – to create the experience of another world, where time and space are distorted, and the mind is temporarily freed from the physical restrictions imposed by the body. But this kind of VR – the future we were promised a decade ago – is uncomfortable, neck-wrenching, vision-blurring, and ultimately unsatisfying. The idea that someday we'll be able to wire our brains directly into the computer and create whatever synthetic realms we might desire has enormous allure, and has captivated minds since William Gibson first wrote about it in his novel *Neuromancer* (1984).

'Cyberspace. A consensual hallucination experienced daily by billions of legitimate operators, in every nation, by children being taught mathematical concepts… A graphic representation of the data abstracted from the banks of every computer in the human system. Unthinkable complexity. Lines of light ranged in the nonspace of the mind, clusters and constellations of data. Like city lights, receding…'

Right from its conception in the pages of Gibson's fiction, cyberspace was always meant to have a game-like quality, a depth and beauty that would make the soul lust for a release from its corporeal imprisonment. Both *Osmose* and *Ephemere* deliver on this promise; many a visitor to these virtual worlds emerges wishing for a more complete unity with the imaginary. For the moment, however, our bodies require that we stand outside our virtual worlds, apart from them. To inhabit these worlds for more than half an hour is to risk permanent damage to one's health.

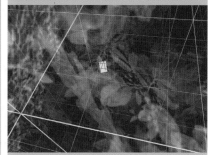

The future does not lie in some synthetic pleasure-world, generated by a computer and projected onto our retinas – at least, not with the technology we know today. Some game enthusiasts look forward to the day when they, like the inhabitants of Ray Bradbury's world in *Fahrenheit 451*, will place the world of simulation around them, in a 360-degree projected panorama. For nearly ten years, the CAVE project at the University of Illinois, Chicago, has been perfecting such an environment, where one can stand in the midst of the virtual world, using screens to supplant the real world. Yet even CAVE, except in a few specific instances, does not satisfy. Realism is arrived at through more than the eyes, or the ears; it's touch, smell and a dozen other sensations and instincts that subtly tell us what is real. Here virtual reality fails us: computers might create a hallucination of the world, but it's other people outside the experience who convince us that the hallucination is real. This is the real drawback of all the VR techniques cooked up thus far by scientists and technologists: they allow for only one person (or at most, a handful) to experience the synthetic simultaneously.

It could well be that, within 20 years, we will have achieved ultimate control over the material world by means of nanotechnology, which would allow us to assemble individual atoms into any desired form. If this becomes possible (and it looks ever more likely), one of its first applications will undoubtedly be to high-end entertainment, and the creation of a virtual theme park that will redesign itself upon demand, according to need or desire. Instead of playing 'capture the flag' on a synthetic landscape, why not duplicate the mountains of Mars using a pile of nano-matter, which, after the game has ended, can recompose itself into a dense jungle for a hunting game? The great advantage of such a development comes not from its nearly infinite flexibility (which introduces a host of ethical concerns, as well, because the imagination run wild can easily run riot), but from its inherently participatory nature. For the first time, many people would be able to participate bodily in the same virtual environment, and people are the 'killer app' of gaming. All attempts to create interesting virtual worlds have faltered because, despite the beauty or interactivity of the environments, they remain among the most isolated places created by man. Until a whole host of humans can inhabit a virtual world at the same time, VR will remain exotic, intellectually stimulating but emotionally empty.

The enormous popularity of *Everquest*, *Asheron's Call* and *Ultima Online* show that, despite clumsy graphics, slow connection speeds and the inevitable medieval storylines, people hunger for games that involve them with other people. We have areas in our brain that are dedicated to helping us model how other people will react to our actions, 'social circuits', which we employ in our day-to-day lives. When these capabilities are engaged in our play, games suddenly acquire a reality beyond the screen, joystick or platform. In South Korea, *Lineage*, an online role-playing game, has become the obsession of over two million people, and many Koreans lead dual lives: a mundane existence in the real world, and an alternative, game-role existence as warrior, magician or commander of a zombie army in the virtual world. It's a Walter Mitty-like state of affairs on a national scale. It seems that, in the future, we'll all be either superheroes or arch-villains.

Opposite page
The CAVE project
NCSA

This page top
Ultima Online

This page bottom
Everquest

✳HEAD GAMES✳

Virtual Reality
Theatre
Institute for Creative
Technologies at
The University of
Southern California

As these massive multi-player online games become a regular feature of life, many of us will reject the flight into a swords-and-sorcery past, or a *Star Trek*-like future of utopian possibilities, preferring instead to focus on the increasing uncertainty of the here-and-now. In this respect, games like Electronic Art's *Majestic* may be the prototype: in the midst of a vast conspiracy, players uncover crucial facts, which, if revealed in time, will save lives, thwart the plot and make them heroes. *Majestic* plays on the hyper-complexity of the modern world with its well-spun conspiracy theories, but exceeds the usual game-playing boundaries, reaching out to the player through electronic mail, telephone, fax, transgressing the now-fading line between the real world of real people and real actions, and the synthetic environment of imagination and play. As the real world becomes more fantastic, so the fantastic world becomes more real.

In the end, all games are head games; we challenge ourselves, our friends and even our enemies to meet us on the battlefields of intellectual effort, physical prowess, diplomacy or brinksmanship. We bloody ourselves in the effort to emerge victorious, and either capture our opponent's flag or go down fighting. Our games are rehearsals for the all roles we're called upon to play in the real world. Even the US army has become fascinated with videogames, funding a new Institute for Creative Technologies to research how to use videogames as training tools for the soldiers of the 21st century. The line between play and combat has never been less clear; before long we may well see the final collapse of the wall that divides the real from the imaginary.

Mark Pesce

Mazzi Binaisa is a freelance writer. She came into contact with games at the age of six, and still hasn't quite got into them nineteen years later. She currently lives in London and is working on her first novel.

J.C. Herz (jc@joysticknation.com) is the principal of Joystick Nation, a research-and-development firm that applies the principles of computer game design to the creation of new products, services, and learning environments. Her book, *Joystick Nation: How Videogames Gobbled Our Money, Won Our Hearts, and Rewired Our Minds*, is published by Abacus (1997).

Henry Jenkins is the Director of the Comparative Media Studies Program at MIT. He is the co-editor of *From Barbie to Mortal Kombat: Gender and Computer Games* and the Principle Investigator for the MIT-Microsoft Games to Teach initiative.

Andreas Lange studied Comparative Religions and Dramatics at Die Freie Universität Berlin. Since 1997 he has been Director of the Computer Game Museum in Berlin, the first museum with a permanent exhibition dedicated solely to interactive digital entertainment culture.

Masuyama (*masuyama@dabb.com, www.masuyama.com*) was born in Tokyo in 1958. He is President of dabb inc. and his current projects include the production of several PC videogames and an exhibition at ICC, Tokyo, entitled 'Credit Game'. He is a Lecturer in Media Studies at Kyoritsu University, Tokyo, and Mukogawa University, Hyogo.

Gautam Narang is a 17-year-old games player. He is Indian, lives in London and loves hip-hop.

Celia Pearce has been designing games, interactive attractions and art projects since 1983. She is the author of *The Interactive Book: A Guide to the Interactive Revolution* (Macmillan), as well as numerous other papers on interactive design, games and narrative.

Mark Pesce is the co-inventor of the Virtual Reality Modeling Language, the author of four books and numerous articles, and was the founding chair of the University of Southern California's New Media Program at the School of Cinema-Television.

Steven Poole is a literary journalist and composer. He is the author of *Trigger Happy: The Inner Life of Videogames* (Fourth Estate, 2000).

Jeremy Relph (*jeremyrelph@hotmail. com*) is a freelance writer based in Toronto. He is currently working on an unauthorized biography of J.J.Flakes: Cereal Kingpin and a collection of short stories entitled *People Get Ready*.

Katie Salen is an Associate Professor of Design at the University of Texas at Austin where for the past six years she has worked with students exploring ideas about design, interactivity, games and play. She lives in Brooklyn and is currently writing a book for MIT Press on game design and interactivity with noted game designer Eric Zimmerman.

Kurt Squire is the Research Manager of the MIT-Microsoft Games to Teach initiative. He is currently finishing his doctoral work in Instructional Systems Technology at Indiana University where he co-founded the joystick101.org.

Alice Taylor is the director of a London-based online entertainment company. She has been an avid fan of gaming since the age of eight, and specializes in hardcore fragging.

Clive Thompson (*clive@bway.net*) is a writer who specializes in the political and cultural effects of technology. He is the technology columnist for *Newsday* in New York, and writes for magazines including *Wired*, *Fortune*, *Entertainment Weekly* and *Shift*.

Eric Zimmerman is a game designer, artist and academic exploring the theory and practice of game design. He is the co-founder of gameLab (*www.gmlb.com*), a game development company based in NYC, and has developed games for CD-ROM, Internet and real-world platforms. He has taught at MIT, NYU and Parsons School of Design, and has published and lectured extensively on game design and game culture.

Numbers in *italics* refer to illustration captions